SAN FRANCISCO

10/16/93
MARLENE AND FRA,
Well at least
SAN FRANCISCO is one
place that you
got before I left –
And fairly often I
might ADD!
It has been a pleasure
having you with us,
this city is one
that we will
have a HARD time
leaving, but just
thinking of you now
have another great place
to Visit!

Pau

ABO

GARDEN
AND
ALTAR OF FREEDOM

eeds divide
d's children

God is not in any
Church or Government

Luther REFORMED and
Pemabo CLARIFIES

World Leaders are all Guilty of

World Peace is overdue!

EVERY DAY 1970

OD + RELIGON
YOUR HEARTS

atholics & Protestants confuse mankind

REWARD
$1000.00

Pemabo
RUTHFUL

The Eternal
City of San Francisco

First Home of United Nations Convention for Peace

Start now Don't wait for Jesus

Mothers hate all WARS

In Memoriam
1776-1970

LIVE and
let live
WITHOUT
W

must reason
top the Bomb!

verge into one Religion

WAR stops
Heaven on earth

alkers are

The BIBLE IS A

Thomas
Paine

Christian
Hypocrit
Bring Wa

Man must learn that-

SAN

FRANCISCO

Photographs by MORTON BEEBE

Essays by HERB CAEN | TOM COLE | BARNABY CONRAD
HERBERT GOLD | JOHN HART | KEVIN STARR

Captions by ALAN MAGARY | ANN SEYMOUR

HARRY N. ABRAMS, INC. | *Publishers*

"A little cable car climbing halfway to the stars," Tony Bennett sings in "I Left My Heart in San Francisco." Cable cars, which haul far more tourists than residents, are nonetheless beloved by most San Franciscans. A guarantee against their abolition was even written into the city charter.

The Golden Gate Bridge takes its name not from its color but from the strait it spans. Comparing it in 1846 to Constantinople's Golden Horn, explorer John C. Frémont wrote, "To this gate I gave the name *Chrysopylae* or Golden Gate."

Fiftieth anniversary celebrations for the Golden Gate Bridge took place in May, 1987. A special feature of these days was that permanent lights were installed on the bridge towers as originally specified in the plans but never carried out.

Tony Sanchez leads students of the Yoga College of India in morning exercises on the Marina Green.

San Francisco's skyline is seen here from above the Bay Bridge's midpoint, Yerba Buena Island.

Cafe singer Bobby Short's musical program *Night of Cole Porter* attracted a gala benefit audience to the foyer of the Opera House, one of the twin War Memorial buildings at Civic Center.

At Christmas the outlines of the Embarcadero Center join the lights of the Bay Bridge and downtown buildings, adding a festive air to the night scene.

San Francisco and the entire Bay area are shown in a remarkable image recorded by an electronic earth scanning sensor known as the Thematic Mapper, which was carried aboard the Landsat 5 satellite. The image was later processed and computer-enhanced on software created by Terra-Mar Resource Information Services, Inc. of Mountain View, California and hardware from Hewlett-Packard.

May brings a burst of cherry blossoms, and a host of visitors, to the Japanese Tea Garden in Golden Gate Park.

"Pemabo" (the late Peter Mason Bond), an artist of the vernacular, shows off his front-yard Peace Garden.

California and Mason intersect atop Nob Hill, a knob where nabobs such as the Central Pacific's Big Four and the Comstock's Bonanza Kings built their less-than-modest dwellings.

A once-controversial landmark, the Vaillancourt Fountain in Justin Herman Plaza (Market at the Embarcadero) now serves as a popular alfresco lunch spot. When dedicated in 1971, the fountain reminded San Franciscans of a Lego set or the ruins of the nearby Embarcadero Freeway.

The entrance of the San Francisco Ballet's stunning new home, designed by Beverly Willis and Associates, captures varying reflective images of the Opera House and City Hall.

Highrise San Francisco: This aerial view from the west shows the Bay Bridge connecting downtown with Berkeley, Oakland, and the East Bay Hills.

INTRODUCTION

Fans arriving for the third game of the 1989 World Series were greeted with a nerve-shattering roar that welled up from the manicured playing field and shook Candlestick Park to its concrete rafters for fifteen terrifying seconds. Across the nation and around the world, television screens tuned to the game shivered and went dark. When they flickered back to life millions of baseball fans became part of the largest audience in history ever to view an earthquake live and in prime time. It was a spectacle, as residents of this irrepressible city like to say, that could only happen here.

For days San Francisco's story led the network news. But while the nation fastened on the details of disaster, San Franciscans focused on rebuilding their city. In no time they were back at work. The gleaming new glass and steel highrises of the financial district were virtually unscathed; most neighborhoods of the city were barely touched. And as the nation shook off the aftereffects of media exaggeration, tourists—one of San Francisco's most important products—overcame their fears and returned to everybody's favorite city.

San Francisco has seen a number of changes since this book appeared in 1985. Each of them, the quake included, has added to the civic exuberance, urban charm, and physical beauty captured so successfully in the first edition. Not satisfied simply to rebuild after the Big One of '89, the city is busily re-creating itself with projects like Santa Fe Pacific's vast new city within a city at Mission Bay. Aging warehouses along the southern waterfront are giving way to attractive housing developments, new restaurants, a sailing center with hotels and shops. Moscone Center, the hub of San Francisco's brisk convention trade, is being enlarged and the surrounding neighborhood transformed. Business thrives. In 1988 and 1989, the city enjoyed the highest rate of successful new business start-ups in the nation.

Capitalizing on historic ties and ethnic diversity, San Francisco aggressively pursues the Pacific Rim trade. It uses the cachet of its championship Forty Niners and Giants to enhance its role as a center of fashion, film production, and video post production. And it never forgets the importance of its varied roots, balancing a richly diverse neighborhood art program and a lively cabaret scene with a firm commitment to a world class opera and a first rate symphony and ballet. No wonder it's everybody's favorite city.

—*Jerry Lubenow*

CONTENTS

HELLO, VISITORS!

BY HERB CAEN

Opposite: San Francisco's weather is often mocked for its summer fog and chill, but it snows once in a blue moon. To make up for that, Financial district workers create a storm of paper on the last working day of the year. The Pacific Lumber Building on Sansome has bay windows that open for natural air conditioning.

Above: After the 1906 fire reduced downtown to ashes and marched south through acres of wooden houses, a humble fire hydrant in the Mission district was miraculously found to connect to an unbroken water main. Firefighters stopped the blaze at 21st Street. Each year on April 18 the hydrant is repainted and garlanded.

Overleaf: Levi Strauss & Company, an important contributor to the city's economy, makes its world headquarters beside a refreshing waterfall and fountain that it created as a public ornament.

Greetings and welcome to San Francisco, city of the world, worlds within a city, forty-nine square miles of ups and downs, ins and outs, and going around in circles, most of them dizzy. A small "d" democratic city run by big-buck conservatives, a place where the winds of freedom will blow your mind and your hat off, where eccentricity is the norm and sentimentality the ultimate cynicism. Cable cars and conventions, boosterism living uncomfortably with sophistication, a built-in smugness announcing simply that we are simply the best. The only city better than San Francisco today was San Francisco yesterday—maybe. Remember, visitors, that you are lucky to be here. Have fun. Spend money. Marvel at our giddy combination of Kookville and High Kultur, busyness and booziness, millionaires stepping daintily over passed-out winos, hot-pantzed ladies of the night throwing themselves at your passing car. Enjoy yourselves, but don't stay too long. Parking is such street sorrow.

Years ago, this wide-eyed kid from Sacramento dubbed it Baghdad-by-the-Bay, a storybook city of spires and minarets, gay banners fluttering in the breeze. A viewtiful city, he called it, a Saroyanesque pastiche of lovable gamblers and boozy bohemians spouting half-aphorisms in saloons run by patrician publicans. The most beautiful bay in the world—only superlatives were accepted—was breasted by ferries that looked like Victorian mansions with sidewheels. Then came the greatest bridges in the world—"the car-strangled spanner" of the bay and Joe Strauss's suspenseful "bridge that couldn't be built." We looked around at the wonderful, funderful city and we were proud to be San Franciscans, the envy of all.

San Francisco, Queen City of the Pacific (the title was once non-ironic), gleaming jewel of the West Coast, surrounded on three sides by water and on the fourth by Republican reality. Occasionally a Republican mayor sneaks in, but it is essentially a city that votes the straight Demo ticket. I don't even know how they get people to run for mayor: who wants to be Chief Kook of Kookville? We have a city father who is an unmarried mother of two and a gay seat on the Board of Supes, as befits the new de-

mographics. San Francisco has a large gay population, and it keeps increasing, although exactly how gays multiply has not been explained. Nothing is ever explained in San Francisco.

"The city that was never a town." There's a thought that appeals to San Franciscans. Will Rogers may or may not have said it, but the phrase does conjure up a flash of the crazed and crazy place that was born in a Gold Rush and grew up overnight to become a fabled city. Tip to visiting journalists: "The coldest winter I ever spent was one summer in San Francisco" was one of the best lines Mark Twain never wrote, but who cares. Whoever said it was accurate enough.

Welcome visitors, to a city as confusing as the Democratic party. If you drive, don't drink, but the driving will drive you to drink. We are casual about street signs, but you might find one if you look hard enough. Directions? Forget it, and don't ask whatever looks like a resident. He won't know either. If you keep going on a one-way street, you will soon come to another one-way street with traffic coming right at you. That's what makes us colorful and our insurance rates the highest. Don't worry about traffic lights. Green and red both mean go like hell; in fact you cross on the green at your own risk. Another tip: No Parking Any Time means park any time, usually on the sidewalk and sometimes on a pedestrian. There are a lot of tow-away zones, so check the signs. It is maddening to pay $60 to ransom your car from a towing company whose slogan is "Discover San Francisco."

San Francisco, a city for all seasons (sometimes four in one day) and various reasons. A city that thinks nothing of spending $60 million to rebuild a cable car system that was obsolete a century ago and even less of letting drunks lie on the street as long as they aren't in the way of the cables; "a sociological, not a police problem," unquote. A city of soup kitchens and two thousand restaurants, some of them excellent and most of them crowded. A place where whites are a minority and "the largest Chinatown outside of the Orient" is no longer large enough. The mayor and both congressmen are Jewish women; do we need a Yenta Control Board?

So welcome, dear visitors, to Crazytown USA. You will either be crazy about it or become as crazy as the rest of us. Either way, may you all return safely to your funny country, that large land mass slightly to the right of Baghdad-by-the-Bay.

Cable cars, San Francisco's moving landmarks, came back to a joyous celebration after a $60 million, top-to-bottom overhaul. Most of the remodeling was to the complex of underground cables and troughs and the power system. A building at Washington and Mason houses the huge electric motor and 12-foot cable winders and bullwheels. *Opposite, above left:* The old wheels were replaced with ones of larger gauge. *Opposite, above right:* Many coats of varnish and paint were applied to keep the rolling antiques shiny. *Opposite, below left:* During the 20-month renovation, a specimen car from the Cable Car Museum perched outside Four Embarcadero Center. *Opposite, below right:* One of the street-long celebrations, this one on Powell Street, looking from the side of Nob Hill south to Market Street.

Overleaf: The cable car welcome included a parade, brass bands, political speeches, and ten thousand balloons released from Union Square. Centered on Union Square are I. Magnin and Macy's, the Hilton, the St. Francis Hotel and its tower, Saks Fifth Avenue, and the Sir Francis Drake, Holiday Inn-Union Square, and Hyatt-Union Square hotel towers.

The small city at the tip of the peninsula is served by many forms of transportation. *Above:* The North Beach waterfront at Pier 39 shares space for shops, yachts, and ferries with a large colony of seals. *Opposite, above:* CalTrain, a state-subsidized Southern Pacific operation, brings Santa Clara and San Mateo commuters into the city. The more extensive BART rapid transit system serves most of the East Bay and, via a tube under the bay, San Francisco. *Opposite, below:* A car climbs through Union Street fog on Telegraph Hill, one of several residential neighborhoods that ban commuter parking.

Above: At Spring Carnival a parade makes its way through the Mission District.

Opposite: Showplace Square comprises two dozen buildings including the San Francisco Gift Center and the Galleria, shown here. The largest carnival celebrated outside Brazil is held annually at Showplace Square.

Union Square: Visitors who want to be in
the heart of things stay at one of the city's
oldest hostelries, the St. Francis (*opposite,
above*). Union Square, the premier
shopping area of the city, is anchored by
such names as Neiman-Marcus, I. Magnin,
Saks Fifth Avenue, and Macy's. Nearby are
Gump's, Tiffany & Co., and Nordstrom.

Overleaf: Opening night of the Opera for
elite San Franciscans is a twenty-four hour
affair that includes luncheons and pre-
curtain champagne suppers in the Museum
of Modern art (here, guests study Nathan
Olivera works), a fashion parade across
the courtyard to the Opera House,
intermission parties, and post-curtain dining
and dancing at several restaurants and
mansions.

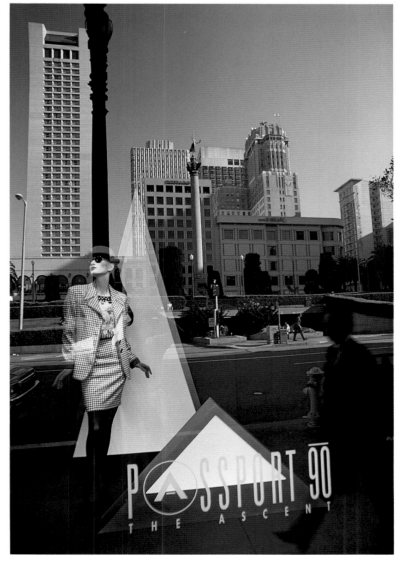

The San Francisco Opera, behind the scenes. *Above:* The wig and makeup departments transform international stars, professional choristers, and San Francisco volunteers (the supernumeraries in crowd scenes) into Russian emperors and Italian peasants, Spanish nobles, and Japanese villagers. *Below:* James Patterson is made up and costumed as Pharaoh in *Aida*. *Opposite:* Spear carriers prepare to march triumphally in *Aida*.

Above: The grand interior of the Opera House, seen here from above the chandelier on opening night. In 1945 the United Nations Conference met here; the charter was signed in Herbst Theater in the adjacent Veterans Building.

Opposite: The Geary Theater, home of A.C.T. (American Conservatory Theater), was built in 1910. A unique baroque building, it was severely damaged during the 1989 earthquake, but is undergoing a magnificent restoration. *Photographs by John Sutton*

Above and opposite: The San Francisco
Ballet performs at Stern Grove, drawing
large and appreciative crowds at these
free, city-sponsored concerts on summer
Sundays.

Golden Gate Park has 1,012 acres of lawn, woodland, flower beds, lakes and ponds, sports grounds, roads, and buildings. Skaters enjoy Kennedy Drive on Sunday afternoon, when cars are banned. Bicyclists—and dogs—use the network of bike paths.

Above: The Conservatory of Flowers at
Golden Gate Park was imported from
Europe by James Lick. It houses tropical
plants, including many species of orchids,
ferns, and water lilies.

Opposite, above: A black-and-white theme
picnic was the winning entry in a contest in
Golden Gate Park. *Opposite, below:*
Similarly attired in black and white are the
penguins at the San Francisco Zoo, having
their own picnic.

At the San Francisco Zoo, hippos Cuddles and Snuggles, mother and daughter, are residents, as is Prince Charles, a rare white tiger (*opposite, below*). *Opposite, above:* The former director of the California Academy of Sciences, Frank Talbot, poses in one of his exhibits. The academy, with museum, planetarium, and aquarium, specializes in Pacific Basin studies.

Opposite, above: Children's Playground at Golden Gate Park comprises four adjoining play areas for kids in different age groups. *Opposite, below:* At the San Francisco Zoo playground, a Plexiglas jungle gym is one of the kid-pleasers.

Above: The Exploratorium is a place where children and adults can learn by exercising the five senses. More than 350 exhibits demonstrate the principles of science, technology, and human perception. There are buttons to push, wheels to spin, levers to pull, objects to touch. In the Tactile Gallery, visitors walk, crawl, sprawl, and squeal through pitch-black darkness on foam rope, velvet, birdseed, and more, led only by the sense of touch. Here, the Bubble Machine is a fascinator. The late Frank Oppenheimer, brother of J. Robert, created the Exploratorium in the hangar-like building of the Palace of Fine Arts in 1969.

San Franciscans turn out for special occasions with celebration and pageant. *Clockwise from lower left:* a jester at Pier 39, the shopping and entertainment wharf; an extravagant party makeup; an appropriately pasta-clad young lady on Columbus Day; a pair of rabbits exchange nuzzles on their way to an Easter party; a float at the Cherry Blossom Festival; and Hispanic celebrants at a Mardi Gras party in the Galleria at Showplace Square.

Overleaf: Denizens of the street include one-man bands and one-man recycling centers.

Veterans of Foreign Wars salute their fallen comrades on Memorial Day at San Francisco National Military Cemetery in the Presidio.

Left: A member of Knights of Columbus is suitably bedecked for a parade on Columbus Avenue on Columbus Day, the Italian-American community's special holiday.

Above: Parading at Japantown's Cherry Blossom Festival are a young Cub Scout with a flagpole in hand and *(right)* a kimono-clad youngster.

Overleaf: A California Street cable car crosses Chinatown's main street, Grant Avenue.

yamato
JAPANESE
RESTAURANT
& Sushi Bar
←

USEUM

ESE
GOODS

AR EAST

CUISIN

FOUR SEA

← 700

CALIFORNIA

琳寬街

NO PARKING
12 MIDNIGHT TO 6 AM
MON. WED. FRI.
STREET CLEANING

LITTER

MARKET ST. CHINATOWN.   NOB HILL &

Souper Star

Chinatown is an island in the city, at once Chinese and American. *Left, above:* A toddler is traditionally costumed in the less-than-traditional Chinese New Year's celebration. *Opposite, above and below:* The biggest street event in San Francisco, the parade features plenty of firecrackers and a multi-person dragon—also all-girl high school glockenspiel bands, dignitaries in antique cars, and Miss Chinatown beauty contestants. *Left, below:* Away from the tourist areas of Chinatown, it is easy for a visitor to feel like a foreigner in Hong Kong.

Overleaf: Open-air cafes are uncommon in San Francisco, but in North Beach those with large plate-glass windows offer good people watching. At right is the Caffé Puccini on Columbus Avenue; top left is Il Fornaio at Levi Plaza; and at bottom left is the Embarcadero's Fog City Diner.

Above: At Tiburon, a ferry ride from San Francisco's Pier 43½, the deck at Sam's serves as a hangout for yachtsmen and tourists.

Opposite: Stinson Beach, because of its gradual slope and shallow, warmer water, is the most popular beach community north of San Francisco.

Left: San Francisco's houses, like those on Telegraph Hill, sometimes seem precariously built because they stand on small, steeply sloping lots. Here, the intrepid walker can climb the Greenwich and Filbert steps to Coit Tower.

Opposite: A cable car creeps up Hyde Street above Aquatic Park. In the background—the Hyde Street Pier and Alcatraz Island.

CITY PERCHED ON A FRONTIER

BY TOM COLE

There will never be another city like San Francisco. At least not until gold or pocketable oil or some rare and delightful thing is discovered on an obscure but gorgeous asteroid and hundreds of thousands of young men—and this time, just maybe, a comparable number of women—cram into rockets and blast off to get rich and build a madcap Plexiglas metropolis. Cities like San Francisco just don't happen anymore. Greed, however happy, has grown more staid. And mass migrations of money drunkards belong to a charming but suspect past.

San Francisco claims to be unique, and it is. It is a boomtown, the very archetype of a tough, loony, and gloriously successful boomtown. And, unlike boomtowns from Alaska to the Brazilian jungle, it lasted, thanks to grace and luck. Its history is dramatic and quirky, but above all it is sudden.

On the morning of the first day of 1848 San Francisco was a boggy, flea-ridden, doubtlessly rather hung-over village. Its fewer than five hundred inhabitants were a miscellany of wanderers, wastrels, and mildly energetic pioneers. One of its leading citizens, a young Mormon named Sam Brannan, had recently writ-

Opposite: Before the bridges were built, the Ferry Building was portal to the city for commuters from Marin and the East Bay.

Right: By all written accounts Yerba Buena in the 1840s was a scruffy place, a robust little commercial village centered on Portsmouth Square. But it quickly absorbed the Presidio and Mission communities, dominated the hinterland, and became the gateway to the Mother Lode.

ten in his newspaper, the *San Francisco Star*, that the village "bid[s] fair to rival in rapidity of progress the most thriving town or city on the American continent."

Brannan's optimism was pure habit. True, the village did sit on the shores of the world's finest anchorage. The visitations of hide-and-tallow ships were becoming more frequent, and the United States of America, having grabbed California from Mexico a few years before, was surely looking westward. But in January 1848 San Francisco was beyond any frontier, nearly as obscure as a dim asteroid. Yet in less than 10 years it would be a world-class dream city with a population it took New York 190 years to reach and Boston 200 years.

San Francisco had a languid history before fortune pounced on it. For four or five thousand years it was the itinerant home of a tribe of gentle Indians the Spanish called Coastanoan, but which are now known as Ohlones. (The Ohlones and the other tribes of the Bay Area, the Carquins and Miwoks, much preferred the more bountiful hills of Marin, Berkeley, and the southern peninsula to the windy, barren, and deeply sandy tip of the peninsula upon which San Francisco now rests.)

The Indians' plentiful existence was ripped apart in 1776 when a Spanish expedition under the leadership of Juan Bautista de Anza encamped on a hill overlooking the Golden Gate and began the colonization of the lands around the stupendous bay. In 1579 Francis Drake had landed his *Golden Hind* somewhere north of the bay (probably at the Point Reyes Peninsula). Drake made a grand but uncharted claim to what would become Northern California. (He called it Nova Albion, and so California can claim to have given its first name to the New England of later years.) The English privateer's claim and, later, the inching of the Russians down the Pacific coast from Alaska irritated Spain, which considered Alta California (the lands north of Mexico) part of its Empire.

By the time de Anza planted a cross at Fort Point and began building a presidio and, a few miles to the south, a mission, Spain's imperial energy was dissipated. The net result of its tired grasping was the discovery of the bay and the utter destruction of the Indians. Much of the drive behind Spain's northward movement had been supplied by priests of the Franciscan order under the stewardship of Father Junípero Serra. Following the practice refined in the earlier missions along El Camino

The self-created legend is a San Francisco characteristic. In 1853 Joshua Abraham Norton nearly made a fortune by cornering the rice market—but went bankrupt and a little mad. Proclaiming himself Norton I, Emperor of the United States and Protector of Mexico, he floated his own banknotes (which were accepted by a few amused restaurateurs) and promoted some mad schemes, including a plan to build a bridge from San Francisco to Oakland. Through the 1860s and 70s he was the city's most notable character. In 1879, the year before his death, he posed for this impressive double exposure.

Real, the Franciscans herded their neophytes into the Mission Dolores, baptized them, and watched helplessly as they died of despair and disease.

When Mexico declared its independence of Spain in 1821, the presidio and mission were little more than empty symbols of Spanish imperialism. The new and impoverished republic attempted to develop Alta California by issuing land grants, and in the 1830s and 40s the hides and tallow produced by those giant land-grant ranches provided the bulk of commerce in and around the bay. But Mexico's hold on Alta California was as tenuous as Spain's, and on July 6, 1846, the American flag was raised over Portsmouth Plaza, the village's hub. America's conquest of California and its absorption into the Union would not take place formally for nearly two years, but the Stars and Stripes, one old settler remembered, were greeted by "the roar of cannon from the ship [the *Portsmouth*], the hurrahs of the ship's company, the vivas of the Californians, the cheers of the Dutchmen, the barking of dogs, braying of jackasses, and a general confusion of sounds from every living thing within hearing."

The doddering village over which the new flag waved was called Yerba Buena, after a "good herb" that grew on the mudflats. Within six months Lt. Washington A. Bartlett, the area's military *alcalde* (mayor), decreed a fateful name change. With an early touch of the self-promotion the city has never lacked, he discarded Yerba Buena for San Francisco, thereby linking the village with the bay. Three hundred and fifty-nine days later a "half-crazy or harebrained" man named James Marshall, poking around in a millrace in the Sierra foothills, made a discovery that would truly create San Francisco and, in the process, change the world.

The California Gold Rush was the consummation of a centuries-old prophecy. Since Columbus happened upon the New World the Spanish had been searching madly for an El Dorado, a land of gold. Other nations had watched or had looked themselves. The English, especially, had been pleased to prey on Spain's gold-heavy ships. But there was never gold enough, and it became part of Western civilization's collective subconscious that a land littered with, bursting with, practically coated with gold was waiting out there somewhere in the asteroid-distant reaches of the New World.

James Marshall found El Dorado on January 24, 1848. He was the mill foreman for John Augustus Sutter, a self-inflated land baron whose "New Helvetia" included a part of the American River near present-day Coloma. The "shiny material" Marshall found at Sutter's Mill was subjected to "every test in the American Encyclopedia" and proved to be the stuff dreams and dream cities are made of. Soon Sutter, Marshall, the mill workers, and rumor-fueled settlers were picking up nuggets by the fistful. And when Sam Brannan paraded a vial of gold dust down Montgomery Street in San Francisco yelling, "Gold! Gold on the American River!" the Gold Rush was on.

It was one of history's greatest mass migrations. Word traveled with whatever speed the times allowed, and within months tens of thousands of bored clerks, lawyers, layabouts, college students, farmers, a few hard-eyed women—even a child or two—were on their way to the land of gold.

There was no easy way to get there. The voyage around Cape Horn was dangerous and long; the route via the Isthmus of Panama somewhat quicker, but sodden and unpredictable; wagon trains across the Great Basin were set upon by cholera, unamused Indians, and ill-entropy. Yet within the first three years of the Rush more than two hundred thousand Argonauts (or 49ers) had arrived in the Golden State. The fabled 120-mile-long Mother Lode was speckled with five hundred or so shanty towns. The world economy was inflated with the gold wrung out of the foothills, America's westward movement was dramatically, inalterably speeded up. California was rushed into the Union, uncountable lives were enriched (by experience, if not gold dust) or cut short, and a hundred-odd miles to the east of the gold country, San Francisco was exploding.

By 1851, the city ranked fourth in foreign trade among America's ports. Its population had grown from that raggedy five hundred to forty thousand, more or less. (Who had the time or inclination to conduct a census?) San Francisco was swilling seven bottles of champagne for every one consumed in Boston. The earliest 49ers had, one New York reporter wrote, "lodged in muslin rooms and canvas garrets with a philosophic lack of furniture and ate [their] simple though substantial fare from pine boards." A few months later "lofty hotels, gaudy with verandahs and balconies, were met with [everywhere], furnished with home luxury, and aristocratic restaurants presented daily their

A forest of masts lined San Francisco's waterfront during the Gold Rush. (This panoramic photograph was taken in 1851 from Rincon Point.) Some of the ships still sailed, but the greater number were abandoned or sold for use as hotels and warehouses in a boomtown continually consumed by fire (1849, 1850—three times, 1851—twice).

long bills of fare, rich with the choicest technicalities of Parisian cuisine."

Physical expressions of San Francisco's boomtown heritage are hard to find today. The earthquake and fire of 1906 destroyed much of the old city, and developers have forever been working their way. On Jackson Street, near the Transamerica pyramid, some old buildings convey a certain Gold Rush charm. The Mission Dolores, much rebuilt, is nonetheless a fascinating relic of the city's colonial past. Yet the tall buildings of today's downtown owe their stability to the mud, abandoned ships, and rocks piled into Yerba Buena Cove to make landfill during the Gold Rush. The very ground an important part of San Francisco rests on is a legacy of the frantic need to fill in the hill-encircled mudflats of the old village-cum-metropolis.

The 49ers were young (most were in their twenties), masculine, and zestful. To most the Gold Rush was the grand adventure of a lifetime and, being a surprisingly educated, even civilized bunch, they self-consciously collected and burnished boomtown tales:

There was the man who cleaned up at the City Hotel barroom. He "would save the sweepings in a barrel, until full; and in washing it he obtained over two hundred dollars."

There was the man who, tea being in oversupply, dumped crates full of the stuff on the tidal flats to make land on which to build a house. By the time his house was finished, the tea in those crates, being in undersupply, was worth "more than a dozen such houses."

There were the $1 eggs, the fortunes lost at the turn of a card, and the "cellar in the earth, twelve feet square and six deep, which rented for $250 a month."

It was a "perpetual carnival" of buying, selling, speculating, getting momentarily rich and grinningly broke. Six deadly fires swept the city in the first few years of the Rush, but each time San Francisco patched itself together and raced on. Prowling gangs like the "Sydney Ducks" or the "Hounds" had to be put down by Committees of Vigilance (the West's first vigilantes). But beneath the daily tumult, the foundations of a great and permanent city were being laid.

By 1853 the river of gold was dropping in its banks. Most of the easily gotten placer gold had been taken out of the foothills. Hundreds of mining towns were collapsing, blowing away into history. But, though its boom slackened, San Francisco was already too established to follow them into obscurity. It was the Queen City of the West, commander of the magnificent bay, funnel for the riches of half a continent.

Yet if it hadn't been for a discovery eerily similar to Marshall's a decade earlier, San Francisco might have settled into something like a comfortable maturity. This time it was silver, not gold, that kindled the boom.

The scraggly denizens of the Virginia Range up near Reno, about 120 miles from San Francisco, had been looking for gold during the past ten years. There was a little up there, enough to buy beans and salt pork for men like Henry T. P. Comstock (who gave his name and little else to the silver district) and James "Old Virginny" Finney (who gave his nickname to the barren boomtown of Virginia City). But the gold was irritatingly mixed up with a dense, bluish clay. In June 1859 that clay was assayed in Grass Valley. Amidst a trace or two of gold was found $3,876 of silver per ton. The Silver Rush, upon which San Francisco would fatten, was on.

Young Samuel L. Clemens was among the first of the troops of young men to assault the Virginia Range and its monarch—the very mountain of silver—Sun Mountain. In his book *Roughing It* Clemens (by the time he wrote it he was known as Mark Twain) confessed "without shame, that I expected to find masses of silver lying all about the ground. I was perfectly satisfied...that I was going to gather up, in a day or two...silver enough to be

Right: Fighting Gold Rush lawlessness was a serious business for the Vigilance Committee members. Many condemned the vigilantes' street justice—it was, after all, lynch law—but in the summer of 1851 it was notably effective against hoodlums: four were hanged, one whipped, twenty-eight deported, fifteen handed over to the police.

Below: Lillie Hitchcock Coit, daughter of an old Carolina family but reared in the best social circles in San Francisco, loved fire engines. A veteran fire chaser, she endeared herself to the volunteer fire companies (some of which were nearly social clubs) and was an honorary member of Knickerbocker Engine Company No. 5. After she died, aged 84 in 1929, her money built two firefighter memorials: Coit Tower and a heroic bronze in Washington Square.

satisfactorily wealthy—and so my fancy was already busy with plans for spending the money."

But Twain and his fellow "almost millionaires" soon found that getting silver out of the mountains was not as simple as sitting by a handy stream while panning and whistling dance-hall tunes. For one thing, there were no streams up in those mountains; long, dangerous, frequently worthless tunnels had to be dug. For another thing, silver required expensive refining. The Silver Rush was a game for capitalists and only a very few lucky claim holders.

The capitalists and the fortunate claim holders were happily located in San Francisco. Virginia City was a "twenty-four hour exercise in bacchanalia," but in the end it was, as Lucius Beebe wrote, "San Francisco's most solvent and essential suburb."

The city's sagging economy ballooned with the riches carried down the mountains by what Twain called an "unbroken... writhing serpent" of pack trains and stages. San Francisco's banks, notably Billy Ralston's Bank of California, became de facto owners of the Comstock district. Ralston built the gargantuan Palace Hotel with silver profits. Four of the luckiest claim holders, the fabled Bonanza Kings—James Fair (of the Fairmont), William O'Brien, John Mackay, and James Flood (his mansion now houses the Pacific Union Club across the street from the Fairmont)—began a mansion-building jamboree atop Nob Hill.

They were soon joined on the heights by the equally fabled Big Four—Leland Stanford (of the university), Charles Crocker

(of the bank), Mark Hopkins, and Collis Huntington (whose eponymous hotels occupy their old mansion sites). The Big Four were the creators of what was imagined would finally ensure San Francisco and California's entry into the grand comity of American enterprise: the transcontinental railroad.

For six years the Central Pacific's laborers—many of them imported from China by Crocker—built the line across the Central Valley and over the Sierra. On May 12, 1869, the Golden Spike was driven at Promontory Point, Utah. The West was finally linked with the East, and in San Francisco it seemed that the last year of a decade had once again brought prosperity.

Instead, the railroad brought unneeded immigrants and

Above: Dining and drinking on the waterfront is a tradition as old as San Francisco. In 1856 one of the famous saloons was Warner's Cobweb Palace, at the head of Meiggs' Wharf (site of the future Fisherman's Wharf). There, Abraham "Monkey" Warner served up hot toddies and crab and clam dishes while presiding in black suit and high silk hat. There he is, eighth from left, with habitués of the waterfront.

Left: San Francisco has not always been a white-collar town. Especially before the earthquake, light to heavy industries ran from the northern waterfront through the eastern part of the city, and the hundred wharves were busy exporting local products. After the local success of the home-built cable cars, San Francisco even made them for other cities—this one for the Second Street Cable R.R. Co. in Los Angeles.

Opposite: Steam engines and horses provided the lifting and pulling power, barrels and boxes the containers, on Green Street Wharf in the early Port of San Francisco. Until the advent of container shipping, the city was a first-class port.

cheaply manufactured Eastern goods. The Central Pacific's Chinese workers—Crocker's Pets, they were called—flooded what was left of the job market, inspiring a decades-long campaign of racism. Union organizers like Dennis Kearney, the "Cicero of the Sandlots," shook their fists at the Nob Hill bosses. When the Comstock's mines began to wilt in the mid-1870s (leading to the collapse of the Bank of California and Billy Ralston's apparent suicide), San Francisco was entrenched in depression.

San Francisco survived its first bout with labor strife and depression in its inimitable boomtown style. What Kevin Starr calls its "intensified pursuit of human happiness" has scarcely ever let up, and may have reached its greatest intensity in the decades before the earthquake and fire of 1906. Rudyard Kipling, visiting during the Gilded Age, called it "a mad city, inhabited for the most part by perfectly insane people."

The Big Four, the Bonanza Kings, and their monied chums entertained in their Nob Hill mansions, whose grand pianos and Greek statues were carried up the hill by cable cars, perfected in 1873 by Scotsman Andrew Hallidie. Those cable cars enabled the city to expand from the old, buried Yerba Buena Cove. It was in this era that the city's Victorian houses were mass-produced. It was the age of the free lunch, of Pisco Punch, and of wicked "French" restaurants. "Drinking," Kipling wrote, "is more than an institution. It is a religion."

It would never attain the ordinary, but as the century turned, San Francisco had polished up some of its frontier roughness. A solid middle class had established itself (though it wasn't until the 1880s that as much as a third of the city's population was female). It was the nation's second port for foreign goods. It had its political bosses and ethnic jostlings, and, as the dislocation brought by the railroad evened out, it linked firmly with the national economy.

San Francisco has always been a city of upheavals, though at 5:12:06 on the morning of April 18, 1906, it suffered its worst. The earthquake shattered a few buildings, broke china heirlooms, and scared the voice out of Enrico Caruso, who was appearing locally in *Carmen*. But it was the fires that almost destroyed the city. They began that morning in the city's center, destroying Billy Ralston's proud Palace, gnawing feverishly at the wooden buildings. Soon a single conflagration spread out from the business district into the neighborhoods, snapping at the heels of fleeing citizens. The fire seethed for two days and three nights until a blessed shift in the wind stopped it on the east side of Van Ness Avenue.

When it was over, more than 250,000 San Franciscans (of a population of about 400,000) were homeless. Five hundred people had been killed and four-fifths of the city's property was in ashes. But it had suffered fires before and its boom mentality ran deep; rebuilding began immediately. As the headquarters city of the West, San Francisco had no choice (and no inclination) but to rush on.

World War I provided a stimulus for San Francisco's renaissance. Just prior to America's entry into the war the city celebrated with the first of its two world's fairs: the extravagant Panama-Pacific International Exposition of 1915. Built on reclaimed land, which today is the Marina, the fair entertained millions of visitors with educational exhibits, titillating arcades, and masterfully designed "palaces" (only one of which, now the Palace of Fine Arts, remains).

Opposite: Arnold Genthe photographed these traditionally dressed girls on "Dupont-gai" (Grant Avenue) at Jackson in pre-earthquake Chinatown.

Earthquake and aftermath: The 1906 quake caused far less damage than the fire, which leveled hundreds of blocks. *Above:* On the first day of the fire, Arnold Genthe captured these well-dressed spectators, standing or sitting politely in chairs on Sacramento near Powell. A day later these houses, too, were gone. *Middle:* On Nob Hill the fire spared only the newly completed Fairmont Hotel and, right, the James Flood mansion (now Pacific Union Club), though both were gutted. The distant tower is City Hall, so shaken that it had to be demolished. *Below:* Much of the city's infrastructure was destroyed, including central phone offices. For several days, telephone operators perched on barrels at the California Electric Works, one of the few large buildings to survive.

Rebuilt, as sassy as ever, San Francisco enjoyed the 1920s in high style. Its bombastic, shiny, perennial mayor (he served from 1911 to 1931), "Sunny Jim" Rolph, presided over a discreetly licentious town. As his old friend Sally Stanford, the city's leading madam, said, "Sunny Jim's motto was 'Don't Stir up Muddy Waters.'" But the Great Depression stirred the waters unmercifully, of course, and once again San Francisco was wrenched with labor hostilities.

At the crucial Port of San Francisco, four thousand longshoremen competed for thirteen hundred jobs parceled out by a shameless company union. Led by Australian-born Harry Bridges, the International Longshoremen's and Warehousemen's Union (ILWU) fought scabs and union busters at the Port on "Bloody Thursday"—July 5, 1934—and then called a citywide general strike, the largest and most successful in American history. When the strike held, union power was firmly established in San Francisco.

Despite the Depression, San Francisco managed to launch two of its (and America's) greatest building projects during the 1930s. In November 1936 the Bay Bridge was opened for traffic, and six months later the lyrical Golden Gate Bridge was completed. The city once again celebrated, this time with the gaudy Golden Gate International Exposition of 1939. The "Treasure Island Fair" (so called for the four-hundred-acre artificial island on which it was built) was gloriously ambitious and mildly scandalous, but like its predecessor, it was stalked by war.

Only the fire and the Gold Rush itself have had as great an effect on San Francisco as World War II. As the major disembarcation point for the Pacific Theater, the city couldn't help but prosper. Shipyards were built all around the bay. Torrents of war workers arrived, sunk roots, bought homes in the city and its expanding suburbs, then raised a generation of children who played prominent, pioneering roles in the tumultuous, exhilarating, postwar decades.

It was in and around San Francisco that the student protests of the 1960s and 70s were spawned; where the beatniks began that historic undermining of the country's complacency; where the hippies prospered and altered America's consciousness; where the New Left flourished and the ecology movement flowered; where—and the city will accept the compliment, however left-handed—new ideas, fads, follies, delusions, and every sweet, and sometimes bitter, untempered expansion of the mind and body find a welcome home. That dim asteroid has a planetary shine, but it's still happiest perched on a frontier.

Above: San Francisco was fortunate in hosting three successful fairs; their sites preserve some delightful remnants. The 1894 Midwinter International Fair—designed to promote the city's remarkably temperate climate—in Golden Gate Park left buildings that became today's M. H. de Young Memorial Museum, the California Academy of Sciences, and the Japanese Tea Garden. The 1915 Panama-Pacific International Exposition—celebrating the completion of the Panama Canal the previous year—left the yacht harbor and Palace of Fine Arts. Its glittering Tower of Jewels on the Avenue of Palms *(left)* had to make way for the houses of the Marina. The last fair was the 1939–40 Golden Gate International Exposition on manmade Treasure Island, celebrating the completion of the two bridges. Its bizarre mix of exotic architectural styles was typified by the Fountain of Western Waters and Court of the Seven Seas *(right).* Its legacy, however, was less durable; the Navy has obliterated all but one of the main buildings and a now-decrepit fountain. *Photo by Roberts & Roberts*

Right: Sutter Street in 1905, when a hundred miles of cable car tracks traversed the city. The cars were built at the Powell Street Cable Car Barn, which still services and makes cable cars that last between sixty and a hundred years for the system.

Middle: The Golden Gate Bridge takes shape, February 1936. Few know that two great bridges were being built about the same time: the 6,450-foot Golden Gate Bridge and the 22,720-foot-long Bay Bridge. The Golden Gate's chief engineer, Joseph B. Strauss, was, interestingly, also a poet and a historical preservationist: he designed the two anchorages on the right to protect old Fort Point, a brick monstrosity that never fired its guns in anger. *Photo by Ted Huggins*

Below: Seen from Sutro Park early in this century is the Great Highway Beach and Playland on the Pacific at the beach end of Golden Gate Park. *Top and bottom photos Courtesy The Maritime Museum.*

Overleaf: Perhaps the city's most famous row of Victorian houses lines Steiner Street at the edge of Alamo Square. These Queen Anne row houses were built in the 1890s by builder Matthew Kavanaugh. A photograph of 1906 shows spectators looking beyond this same row of houses to the Financial district burning in the background.

A SYMBOL OF CIVILITY

BY KEVIN STARR

Opposite: Transamerica Corporation wanted a perfect pyramid for its headquarters, but architect William Pereira of Los Angeles had to add "ears" to accommodate elevators and other utilities; the aluminum spire is mostly hollow. The once-controversial building has since become a distinguishing element on the city's skyline.

Above: Devotees of "street furniture" will spot several varieties of ornamental streetlights downtown. Architect Willis Polk and sculptors Arthur Putnam and Leo Lentelli designed the three-light standards on Market, and these two-light standards on Post, Sutter, and other shopping streets.

Struggling by as a tiny Hispanic outpost for the first sixty-odd years of its existence, the Mexican village of Yerba Buena found itself, by 1870, the tenth largest city in the United States. And it was thus—as the premier city of the Far West—that San Francisco continued through the first century of its American existence. With the exception of Chicago, there was literally no major urban competitor to San Francisco until the rise of Los Angeles in the 1920s. Omaha and Denver, after all, remained relatively small railroad towns through most of the nineteenth century; and Los Angeles was only hovering around the fifty thousand mark at the century's turn.

This urban isolation conferred on San Francisco that self-consciousness which is characteristic of maritime urban colonies. To the east of San Francisco extended the vast and relatively unsettled Far West and the midwestern states. To the west extended the vast Pacific, where only the sketchiest of American traces might be found in those early years. Like the Greek cities of the Mediterranean, San Francisco developed as both autonomous in its isolation and yet possessed in its art, literature, architecture, and civic life of the high forms of urban experience.

Here was a city which by the 1880s had built for itself the largest hotel in the Western Hemisphere, one of the largest opera houses, a glorious public park (the Golden Gate Park), a series of magnificent churches and synagogues, a fully functioning research academy of sciences, and a series of private mansions (for the Crockers, the Stanfords, the Hopkinses, the Floods, and others), as if it were already the capital of a settled Far West. As late as the first decade of the twentieth century, in fact, nearly seventy percent of the population of California lived in the vicinity of the San Francisco Bay Area. The fact is: San Francisco developed out ahead of the frontier, energized by a civic maturity and energy far in excess of its surrounding provinces.

Today, in the 1980s, that hegemony has been lost. Greater Los Angeles, for one thing, encompasses some nine million souls; and San Diego and San Jose each surpass San Francisco in population. The grand city of the Pacific, once so splendid in its isolation, now carries on its existence as one small city-county, with slightly more than seven hundred thousand residents, set in the midst of an urban/suburban continuum bordering the bay that approaches the six million mark in population. Omaha, Denver, Seattle, Las Vegas, Phoenix—the Far West and the Southwest are today dotted with urban concentrations rivaling San Francisco in population, power, and authority.

Nowhere has this fact of competitive urbanism been more apparent than in the San Francisco Bay Area itself. At the southern edge of the bay, San Jose, a sleepy agricultural community through the 1950s, has been transformed in the past two decades into the third largest city in California, administrative capital of high technology. Once dormant suburbs such as Palo Alto, Mountain View, Sunnyvale, and Santa Clara have grown collectively into Silicon Valley, the nerve center of the high-tech electronics industry in the United States. On the eastern edge of the bay, a vast new city—called Contra Costapolis by the *San Francisco Chronicle*—has now reached the three million-plus mark and continues to grow as communities such as Concord, Walnut Creek, Lafayette, and Moraga coalesce with the existing urban fabrics of Berkeley, Kensington, Oakland, Alameda, Fremont, and Union City to form an emerging rival to whatever claim San Francisco still holds as capital of the Bay Region.

And yet, the psychological and cultural center of this megalopolis, extending from San Jose in the south through Marin County to Santa Rosa in the north, is still the City of San Francisco. Like the City of London set in a few square miles of greater London, the City of San Francisco still preserves and keeps energized the civic symbols of the Bay Region. In spite of its losing battle against comparative statistics, San Francisco still remains the one definable urban archetype, set strategically on the edge of an astonishingly beautiful peninsula, jutting into an incomparably beautiful bay. It is not uncommon for residents of San Jose or Santa Rosa, Alameda or Kentfield, to identify themselves when traveling, first and foremost, as San Franciscans.

First of all, San Francisco maintains an ethnic diversity unmatched in the suburbs. There is literally not one definable segment of the human family unrepresented in the San Francisco population. Indeed, one can read the history of migration to this country successively backwards in time merely by cataloging the most recent arrivals to San Francisco: from the Vietnamese,

Opposite: A loggia of considerable proportions fronts the new Federal Reserve Bank, designed by Skidmore, Owings & Merrill, on Market Street.

Overleaf: The Financial district's boxes and cylinders are capable of a little magic at sunset. *Left:* The Wells Fargo Building and an older neighbor, 111 Sutter Street, are lit up. *Right:* The glass facets on Philip Johnson's serrated tower, 101 California Street, reflect and refract the afternoon sun.

Cambodians, and Laotians, who are now busy transforming the downtown Tenderloin district into a mini-Saigon; to the Filipinos and Samoans who began arriving in great numbers in the 1960s and who now have risen to prosperity as homeowners in the southwestern portion of the city; to the Irish—the last major wave of Irish migration to America—who came in the immediate postwar period, joining the more than one hundred thousand Irish already in the city. From this perspective, the influx of gay Americans into San Francisco becomes not an exception to the pattern of migration, but part of a larger process: for this group as well has come to San Francisco in search of better days and opportunities, for that special quality of personal freedom—the ability to define yourself on your own terms—that is so much a part of the San Francisco gestalt.

When one considers the older immigrants to the city—the Irish, the Italians, the central-European and eastern-European Jews, and the white Anglo-Saxon Protestants of every description—one encounters a unique immigration experience. Unlike the more established cities of the East, no one group came into San Francisco and established dominance. The post-frontier elite of San Francisco displayed an unusual interplay of Catholic, Protestant, and Jewish themes. So much so, in fact, that many visitors from the East, when first encountering the First Families of San Francisco, confess a certain surprise at the ecumenism of the local establishment. Sephardic and German Jewish names, for instance, adorn civic institutions—museums, parks, aspects of the musical and artistic establishment—as living proof that pioneers of every persuasion made it big in frontier San Francisco and moved from success to philanthropy.

Whatever else San Francisco has been, it has not been a very wise city—neither in the nineteenth century nor at present. The experience of San Francisco has been from the start a headlong rush to the future—not the sorting and reflection that characterize a high urban civilization in its ripest phases. Notice how few philosophers or systematic thinkers this city has produced in its one hundred years of American history, and how we have lost those we did produce—Josiah Royce, Henry George, for instance—to the East. Even today, outsiders discern a certain glib gossip-column superficiality in our downtown utterance and behavior: a preference for the derivatively chic over true urbanism that is, like Samuel Johnson's London or Tolstoy's Moscow,

Opposite, above: The elegant Mandarin Hotel sits perched atop the First Interstate Building, whose twin towers, a recent addition to the skyline, are popularly referred to as the "tweezers."

Opposite, below: A new San Francisco has risen on the site of the old produce market next to the Embarcadero at Market Street. Here, One, Two, and Three Embarcadero Center, with the cross-braced Alcoa Building at the lower right.

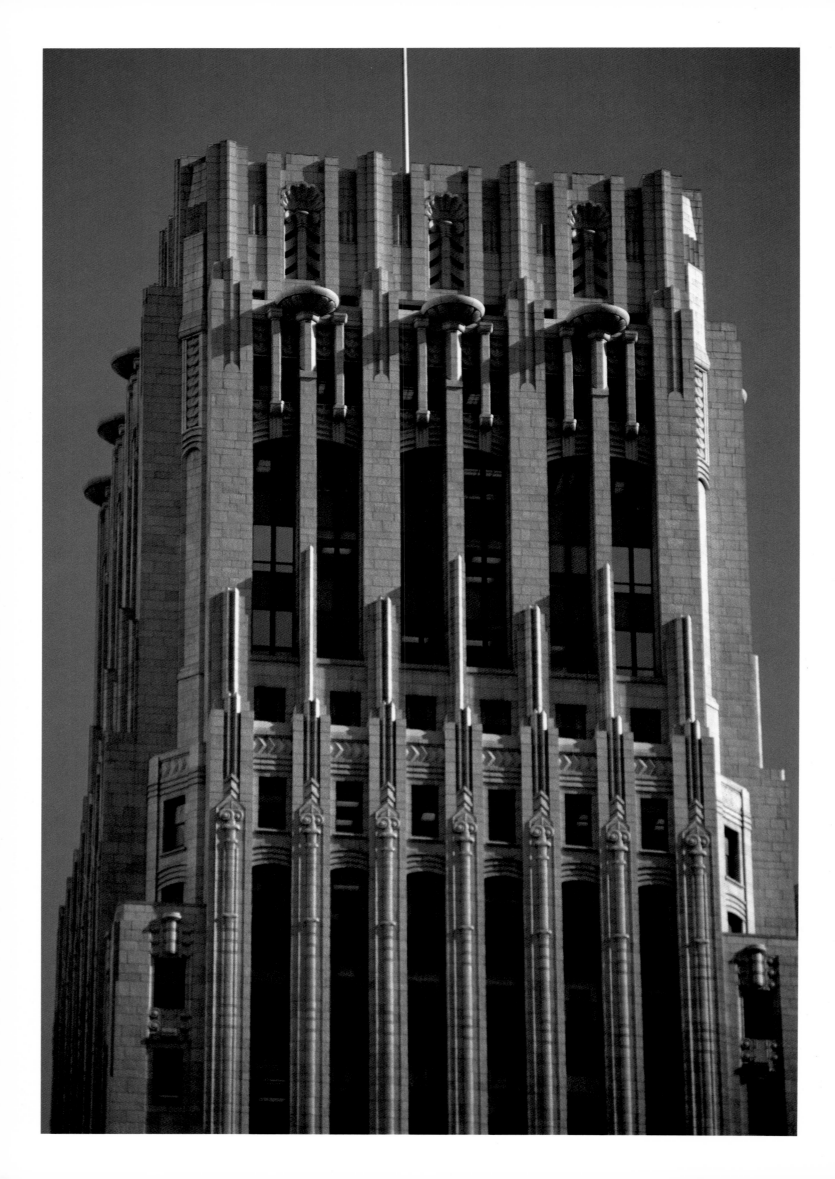

Opposite: With the Pacific Coast Stock Exchange, San Francisco tenuously holds the sobriquet "Wall Street of the West" despite the greater concentration of money and power in that upstart in the southland, Los Angeles. Miller & Pflueger's extensive 1930 remodeling of a 1915 building shows early Moderne touches.

Above: Fog and sun have a transforming effect on the top stories of the Bank of America World Headquarters, a building that dominates the skyline as the bank dominates finance in the West. The 52nd-floor Bankers Club by day becomes the Carnelian Room by night.

107

often embarrassingly groping and clumsy in its pursuit of the true, the beautiful, and the transcendent. San Francisco has a tendency to bluff its way through mystery and tragedy with quips, one-liners, verbal bric-a-brac, and gossip—feeling itself a clever, clever city when it is at its best, behaving like walk-on parts in a forgotten novel by Gertrude Atherton.

And yet the obverse side of this naive catholicity is tolerance. It may be San Francisco's greatest wisdom—a wisdom diffusely shared by the entire city—that it is tolerant: that it does not prematurely judge, that it performs a work of experiment for the entire nation. The nineteenth century saw the labor movement begin here with the Workingman's Party—and the eight-hour day. The twentieth century has seen the city contribute significantly—for better and for worse—to the cultural revolution we have just been through. Perhaps San Francisco's wisdom is not the wisdom of prudence, but of innovation; not the work of retrospective speculation, but active, headlong experiment.

If so, then the risks are apparent: the discard rate of the city—the using up of ideas, styles, values, institutions, and people—proceeds at too headlong a pace. The city devours too quickly, and half-digests.

Yet the advantages are as apparent as the risks. The city continually renews itself, submitting its orthodoxies to the bracing challenge of new thought, opening itself to new people, new races, new cultures. Taking such risks, it embarks upon a work of reconciliation and healing of diverse peoples' values and opinions which a city like Boston, for instance, so venerable in its history and adroit in its culture, has not been able to do: Boston, torn by class conflict and ideological warfare, in a way we hope San Francisco shall never be.

Perhaps San Francisco's wisdom now gathers strength beneath the surface of its present distress and confusion over the question of proper growth: a wisdom based upon the recognition that for all its faults, for all the problems that assault the present, San Francisco is, quite frankly, a masterpiece of human creation. Whatever the tragedies or injustices of the past, whatever the inequities or unfinished business of the present, nature and human action have bestowed upon San Francisco a tone and style and surpassing loveliness: a city so fine in its total, physical self, in fact, that it is in itself an achieved symbol of its own best suggestions. San Francisco is a city of human scale and

Above, and at right: The landmark Garden Court of the Sheraton Palace Hotel has been the site of countless debutante parties as well as more mundane luncheons since 1875. Built by banker William C. Ralston, the Palace has hosted emperors, kings, and presidents. The Garden Court survived the 1906 earthquake, which destroyed the rest of the hotel, and it was incorporated into the new structure in 1909. Eight decades later the hotel underwent a $135 million restoration.

accessibility; a city of site and climate and diverse human stock; a city cherished as a symbol of civility.

What is a city anyway—this or any city, small or great? A city, Aristotle tells us, is a place where men and women come together to become more human. A city, Lewis Mumford points out, is both the substance and the symbol of mankind's communal self. We founded cities—Ur, Jerusalem, Athens, Chicago, San Francisco—so that we might fill out for each other what is lacking in each other's lives; as a matter of business and spirit, art and family. We came together in cities—in some dawn time—so that we might cooperate with each other in the work of living, in the joy of creativity, in the struggle for transcendence. No wonder, then, that the great religions of the world so frequently turn to the image of the heavenly city as the symbol par excellence of achieved human felicity.

That heavenly city, the ideal city beyond time, haunts our collective imagination. St. John the Divine saw it, for instance, as "pure gold, like unto clear glass." Our expectations, of course, are less exalted; and yet even the most realistic of us might hope for a renaissance of shared community, for a return to cooperative urbanism. Purely practical struggle, without vision and community, soon descends to fatiguing factionalism, argument and quarrel for their own autistic sake. The present sectionalism of San Francisco, its infinite multiplication of competing interest groups, is valuable as a first stage of consolidation. The next stage—that of cooperation and broad civic concern—is much more interesting and important.

In 1906, San Franciscans rebuilt their city on their own resources and energies. That was the city's second founding—after the frontier. The third founding lies ahead. It is neither arrogant nor pretentious to say that San Francisco is now embarked upon an ordeal of transformation and survival. Government, business, labor, property owners, and even the alienated must internalize some sense of shared human fate, or else faction will breed faction until the city is destroyed once again in an even more deadly conflagration than that of 1906: a fire of social conflict that will make an ash heap of the city's soul and end once and for all that subtle, but palpable tradition of civilized urbanism, which, along with the gift of natural beauty, has made San Francisco appear to the eyes of the world a city bathed in grace and light.

Opposite, above: On the Symphony's opening night the old lady across the street—City Hall—peeks through the windows.

Opposite, below: In 1964 William Matson Roth, heir of a shipping fortune, transformed a confusion of derelict chocolate-factory buildings into a glittering architectural jewel called Ghirardelli Square. The factory's sign has been a beacon for mariners for a century.

Above: Flowers enliven a Union Street shopping scene.

Left: The Crocker Galleria is a new shopping arcade in the Financial District.

Opposite: After a ferocious battle that delayed the project five years, architect Philip Johnson reluctantly incorporated the white-glass dome and rotunda of the turn-of-the-century City of Paris department store in his 1981 Neiman-Marcus building.

Downtown comes perilously close to marching up Nob Hill and over it. *Above, left:* The French community's church, Notre Dame des Victoires, holds its place on the Pine Street slope. *Above, right:* One of the few private houses on the crest of the hill is this bijou townhouse at 1172 Sacramento, extensively remodeled from 1908 flats. *Opposite:* The wedding-cake Chambord Apartment House was stripped of its ornaments in the fifties, almost demolished in the seventies, but restored as an architectural confection in the eighties. An electric trolley bus passes in the foreground.

The city's Victorian houses—Italianate, Stick, Queen Anne—have come back with a flourish. An abundance of durable, easily shaped redwood made San Francisco a city of wooden houses—brick and stone are uncommon materials. Even the humblest flat-fronted cottage could echo a grand Victorian house and sport a fancy cornice. After the turn of the century Victorians were regarded as impossibly old-fashioned. But beginning in the 1960s, dedicated new owners peeled off stucco, tore down false walls, reapplied custom woodwork, and commissioned multi-hued paint jobs. The largest collections of Victorians are in the Mission, Noe Valley, Eureka Valley, Western Addition, and Pacific Heights neighborhoods. Bay windows are such a trademark of residential architecture that city planners have

now mandated them on most new houses. *Above:* The owner of this Pacific Heights mansion until recently rotated his collection of teddy bears in front windows. *Opposite, above right:* This square-towered 1889 mansion facing Alamo Square was once the scene of White Russian emigré gatherings—thus its nickname, "The Russian Embassy"; under its current name, Warner Embassy serves as a bed-and-breakfast inn.

Overleaf: From Golden Gate Park's highest point (412 feet), Strawberry Hill, the neighborhoods often called "The Avenues" stretch out over the former sand dunes all the way to 48th Avenue and Ocean Beach. In the foreground, the Sunset district.

The southern area of the city comprises districts like Crocker-Amazon, Outer Sunset, Bay View, and Silver Terrace, and shopping areas like Ocean Avenue, Taraval Street, and San Bruno Avenue. Southern San Francisco is also where half the San Franciscans live. *Above:* The southern neighborhoods are, interestingly, where developers followed the terrain when laying out streets and lots. This aerial view looks east over the city. *Opposite, above:* San Francisco State University *(lower edge)* and Park Merced's apartment towers look south to Daly City. *Opposite, below:* Streets ring Mt. Davidson, at 938 feet the highest in the city. By contrast, Telegraph Hill is only 284 feet, Nob Hill 376.

The Palace of Fine Arts reminds San Francisco of the 1915 Panama-Pacific International Exposition. Bernard Maybeck's stucco-faced lath-and-plaster pavilion on a lagoon was a hit. While the rest of the fair site became the Marina, the Palace was saved, and was completely rebuilt of cast concrete in the sixties. Now it serves as a popular site for weddings, advertising photographers, and picnickers.

Opposite: Three thousand voices are raised to the heavens, or at least to the roof, of Davies Symphony Hall in the annual sing-a-long "Messiah."

Above: Frolicking atop Nob Hill is rare, except for this statue in Christmas-lit Huntington Park. On the right stands Grace Cathedral and its chapter house. The park occupies the site of C. P. Huntington's mansion, Grace Cathedral the site of Charles Crocker's; both were destroyed in 1906.

Overleaf: Although the Transamerica pyramid and the Bank of America building have become San Francisco landmarks, the skyline of the city during the past twenty years has seen nearly continual change. The city's planning commission, however, now encourages lowrise building.

Above: Golden Gate Park's Conservatory is a sparkling copy of one in Kew Gardens, outside London. It was a bequest of the eccentric philanthropist James Lick, who had intended it for his Santa Clara farm.

Opposite: Sunset illuminates the oldest of San Francisco International Airport's three terminals, the Central, recently remodeled for international arrivals. Established in 1927 as Mills Field, "SFO" is one of the Bay Area's largest employers.

Overleaf, left: On Market Street, Shaklee Terraces, headquarters of the health-products company, is a silverized update by Skidmore, Owings & Merrill of the International Style. Beyond it is 101 California. *Overleaf, right:* At Columbus and Montgomery, the Transamerica Pyramid (1972) and the Sentinel Building (1905) each make an interesting point.

Above: Options trading at the Pacific Stock Exchange begins early in the morning to keep up with New York hours.

Opposite, above: The carousel at Children's Playground in Golden Gate Park has been painstakingly restored for a new generation of riders.

Opposite, below: Lombard Street takes eight turns among the hydrangeas on its one-way route from Hyde down Russian Hill to Leavenworth. The Powell-Hyde cable car stops at the top for photographers and brave pedestrians. Potrero Hill has the other crooked street— Vermont from McKinley to 22nd Street— but that makes only five full turns and two half-turns. Neither is the steepest street: that honor is shared by 22nd Street between Vicksburg and Church, and Filbert between Hyde and Leavenworth, both a 31.5-degree grade.

Overleaf, left: The television tower on Mount Sutro soars higher than anything else in the city—sometimes even above the fog banks that push up against Twin Peaks.

Overleaf, right: An aerial view of the Marina district shows where some of the most severe damage resulted from the effects of the 1989 quake.

Above: Statues outside this Pacific Heights
mansion turn to peer inside.

Opposite: Stucco houses built in the 1920s
to 1950s stand cheek-by-jowl throughout
the somewhat flat western districts of the
city. The Sunset, Richmond, Parkside, and
other neighborhoods are often called "The
Avenues" (2nd to 12th, 14th to 48th).

Above: On Battery Street, a terraced walkway passes the restored Federal Reserve Building, now the home of a private corporation, and the Park Hyatt Hotel.

Opposite: "That eyesore—which looks like an incinerator," novelist Gertrude Atherton termed Coit Tower. But residents of North Beach, the village neighborhood at its base, couldn't do without their tower of light.

Opposite: Christmas lights define the graceful outlines of Embarcadero Center.

Above: Architect John C. Portman, Jr.'s concrete sculpture "The Tulip" at Four Embarcadero Center is one of the many pieces of public art at the office-shopping-restaurant complex; in the background is the Ferry Building, with its brilliant night lighting.

Overleaf: Thunder and lightning storms are rare in the generally moist Pacific Coast skies. From the northern waterfront, Angel Island appears to the right.

Above: China Basin, site of the newest yacht harbor in the city, stands at the terminus of the never-completed freeway 280.

Opposite: The Ferry Building, centerpiece of the Port of San Francisco, survived the 1906 earthquake and the "nearly big one" of 1989.

SAN FRANCISCO AS PART OF THE REAL WORLD

BY HERBERT GOLD

Opposite: Steve Silver's revue *Beach Blanket Babylon* is one of the city's longest-running entertainments. The hats worn by singers tower eight feet or more, expand, light up—do everything but serve drinks.

Top: The San Francisco Mime Troupe, survivor of a more politically activist era, still presents political satires; this one at Ghirardelli Square. *Above:* A summertime diversion takes place across the Golden Gate Bridge at the Renaissance Pleasure Faire, where Elizabethan—and other—costumes are encouraged.

Vigilantes to Dr. Lovejoy, a San Francisco conman:
"Is there anything you'd like to say before you're hung?"

Dr. Lovejoy: "Not at this time."

San Francisco is famous for running a hundred-year-old operetta for the entertainment of itself, visiting sailors, and other tourists and conventioners. The sets include North Beach (Italian jollity and cappuccino), the Tenderloin (ambisexual lower depths), Chinatown (souvenirs, restaurants, and an occasional gang rumble), Fisherman's Wharf (seafood, sea smells, and bongo players), the Haight-Ashbury (a now-gentrified counter-culture), the Castro (Shangri-la for homosexuals), Nob, Russian, and Telegraph Hills (worn elegance), Pacific Heights and Union Street (spanking-bright elegance and singles shopping); the characters include beatniks, hippies, ethnics of black, brown, yellow, and pink hues, and a large supporting cast of prospering runaways from less clement climes. There are also the Old Families, who have been here more than twenty minutes and have made their money in banking, insurance, mining, railways, land, or politics. Or in the manufacture of jeans. There are the cute and the less cute crazies. San Francisco is America's Pigalle and Saint-Germain-des-Prés, if not its Paris.

The above exaggerations are not fair to the case, of course, any more than it's fair to say that Washington, D.C., is merely government. But it's also part of the truth, isn't it?

A walking town, blessedly limited and cleansed by the bay and ocean, San Francisco is also America's last great metropolitan village. It is a place to be explained, like the blind man defining an elephant—different wherever you happen to touch it. Let us stipulate, before dealing in its oddnesses, that it is also a city like any other middle-American place—a union town, a place of residential neighborhoods and watered gardens and kids playing, the Richmond, Sunset, Mission, and Noe Valley districts. While middle- and working-class people who attend PTA meetings occupy most of the city, the few blocks along Valencia that form a kind of lesbian nation are more likely to attract attention. And perhaps this is as it should be, since exceptional laboratories and resorts are appropriate for visitors, who, after all, are seeking to break out and Make It New, temporarily.

San Francisco's provincial pride and self-importance are reminiscent of other places with a historical vision of themselves, such as Boston, Chicago, or New Orleans. Yet nobody came first; it was a place of a few hundred frontiersmen until the Gold Rush, a mere 130 years ago. I once heard the publisher of the *San Francisco Examiner*, the former flagship of the Hearst newspapers—now struggling against the mighty *Chronicle*, an entertaining daily magazine—praise Kenneth Rexroth during a testimonial dinner to the distinguished old literary man: "He is a great poet, a great critic, and one of the *San Francisco Examiner*'s finest columnists." Self-reference is one of San Francisco's habits, like the beautiful woman who has a few nagging doubts. A front-page story in the *Chronicle*—on a day when sieges of the British and Libyan embassies in London and Tripoli, mining of Nicaraguan ports, political campaigns, perturbations in the economy, and the unbalanced budget were the big news in other newspapers—concerned the crusade by Warren Hinckle to change the city song from Tony Bennett's "I Left My Heart in San Francisco" to the "San Francisco" made famous by Jeannette MacDonald in a Clark Gable earthquake movie. The first sounds like a ditty about an item forgotten in a hotel room, but the second reminds people of the earthquake past and, more important, to come.

This is not an unusual controversy for the *San Francisco Chronicle*, which through the years has served the region by exposing the defects of restaurant coffee, has explored the local beatnik and hippie philosophies, and has featured the columnist

Opposite, above: Yamaha scooter enthusiasts convene atop Twin Peaks.

Opposite, below: The downwind leg of an evening race sponsored by the Sausalito Yacht Club.

Above: The "Letho Hill Mob," from an East Bay club, wheels through Golden Gate Park during a Fourth of July parade. *Photo by Katia Beebe*

Opposite: For the second time in four years the San Francisco 49ers won the Super Bowl, this time as the "home team" at Stanford University Stadium. Coach Bill Walsh and quarterback Joe Montana put together victories over the Cincinnati Bengals in 1982 and the Miami Dolphins in 1985. The city has always been mad for the 49ers, less enamored of the hapless baseball Giants and the Warriors basketball team.

Herb Caen's witty and bemused view of the scene for more than forty years. A typical *Chronicle* lead might read: "Ten thousand drug-crazed, bottle-wielding hippies failed to appear this morning at City Hall."

Boxes selling *The New York Times*, *USA Today*, *The Wall Street Journal*, and other newspapers have been implanted all over town, but the proud *Chronicle* retains a firm grip on the spirit of the place.

Recently I met an immigrant to San Francisco, a former editor of *Harper's Bazaar* who found herself at this frontier after a divorce. Knowing herself to be canny, shrewd, disabused, très East Coast, she was properly suspicious of the trendy Bay Area. "I hate all these cults and fads," she said, "est, Dianetics, Bubba Free John, Synanon, Muktananda, Eckankar, Sri Rajneesh, Baba Ram Dass, all those phonies—you know?"

"I know."

She tapped a pencil to her exquisite nose (a little more exquisite than the one she used to have). She was ready to share something with me. "Only one of those groups is any good. It's my Tuesday evening Affluence Visualization Seminar. I used to have a problem about getting rich, really visualizing it, you know, so I was stuck at the bourgeois level. I didn't appreciate myself, but now I'm up for it and it's happening."

"You mean your class helps you to get along with being rich or it helps you to get money?"

"Both. My problem was both. It was my anima. Affluence Visualization is a combination of the best in Arica, Zen, Jung, and our leader's own discoveries about how you really see it in your own heart and mind—he's beautiful. A karma like you wouldn't believe. Used to be a super ad man, but he dropped out because he really visualized being a tycoon in the field of helping people."

The lady was overcome by the mood of the Bay Area—define yourself, make yourself whatever you want—but she is fulfilling her dream with a little Gesture for Success business, a boutique-improvement enterprise. Trendiness is a persistent trend in this climate where it is forever springtime. When I came out to live in San Francisco twenty-five years ago, I discovered that you never had to wonder whether or not to open or shut the window—the weather was okay. You didn't have to rush out to en-

Opposite, above: The annual Bay to Breakers race attracts serious runners as well as fun-loving joggers and walkers from all over the Bay area. Many participants wear costumes and some run in groups.

Opposite, below: On Angel Island, runners warm up for a race sponsored by the Guardsmen, business and professional men who raise money to send disadvantaged boys to camp.

Overleaf: Baker Beach, on the Pacific side of the Presidio, hosts an occasional sand sculpture contest.

joy a good day; most days are good. It was nice to work in a place where the climate is a friend. There are enough adversaries elsewhere in the world.

But perhaps ease has a price in the emphasis on food, comfort, style, and making out okay. A bookstore owner reports that a San Francisco matron, planning a trip to Europe, came in to ask for George Orwell's *Dining Out in Paris and London*. A high school girl in a literature class, studying Shakespeare's *Romeo and Juliet*, wrote in her paper that Juliet spoke to Romeo from her "deck." A perhaps apocryphal advertisement on behalf of a progressive couple: "Seek to adopt a gay baby."

There are rent-a-dream businesses, cars for that special date, maybe dates for that special car. Celebrities are for lease. A couple I know stages parties with themes for people who want to live out their fantasies. In my jeans and boots I attended a beatnik party for a violinist celebrating his sixtieth birthday: he remembered that he was young and full of vibrato in the fifties. Other themes offered: first-class ocean liner, tennis-anyone, and, of course, that quaint old standby—the orgy. There is also a lawyer who can make you into a fairly genuine bank president for a small fee. He sets up the papers; you now own a bank, or at least a postal deposit box with a banklike name, on some charming Caribbean island.

All of this smoke and fume exists in every American place, even in my hometown of Cleveland—where I find a mini-San Francisco in the Coventry–Euclid Heights Boulevard neighborhood—but the concentration is richer here. A few people jog in Cleveland; a horde of running executives stake out their territory in the City and County of San Francisco. They fight traffic instead of lunch downtown during the midday. They streak past tourists, delivery trucks, outdoor food wagons, bicyclists with propellers on their cute messengers' heads. Old San Francisco is the backdrop for these aerobic anti-cholesterol achievers, loping and roaming past the new high-rise sites, working out their primeval animal rebirth. During the sunny or foggy business days of the city it's an inspiring vision of optimism. New office suites are being built with showers. The rest of us are playing squash or racquetball.

I used to describe the street life of San Francisco as a carnival. Operetta now seems more appropriate, although there are some hazards in street crime, transvestite hookers, a diverse out-

Now the largest daytime parade in San Francisco, the Gay Freedom Day march is a colorful revel in a city known for boisterous and unorthodox celebrations.

patient population—junkies, geriatrics, alcoholics, recent immigrants from Southeast Asia, halfway house lodgers, sexual outlaws, motorcycle and leather people—and even a few bohemians stacked among the porn houses, racketing bars, used book and record and clothing and food stores in the Tenderloin, near several of the city's major hotels. A few days ago, walking to the Press Club, I saw a man waving his wallet, out of which money was leaking, at a stiletto-heeled person who was either a man or a woman: "Hey! You dropped your hook!"

As I passed him, he was muttering compassionately, "A hooker needs her hook."

Yet even the Tenderloin is a neighborhood with a certain dead-end animation and energy. Funky psychedelic murals, like prehistoric cave paintings, are fading into history in stores that used to sell "paraphernalia" and now house bewildered Southeast Asian tribespeople. Jane Jacobs, in her book *The Life and Death of Great American Cities*, listed San Francisco's North Beach as one of the great American neighborhoods, along with Greenwich Village and a part of Boston that has been mostly redeveloped since. North Beach, despite topless dancing, still carries on the tradition of the Barbary Coast. But the long-running operetta has also spawned new strolling and eating-out and cafe-sitting neighborhoods all over this town that is so energetically devoted to pleasure: Russian Hill has cafes, and Clement has become an auxiliary Chinatown, and Potrero Hill has leaned a small bohemia against its Greek, Thai, and White Russian community. The Haight has revived, there are espresso machines and bookshops out near the various art cinemas on Irving and Chestnut and Union Streets. Discretionary income, time, and energy are among the deals that come with forever-springtime. Not many people are artists and philosophers, yet the cafes and streets seem to be full of them. Those who like the town a lot (of whom I am usually one) might describe it as a medieval city with marketplaces and life expended in raucous public, a Mediterranean port with a history—albeit a short one—enclaves of defined neighborhoods, variety, fun, sunlight, fog. Those who like the city less (of whom I am also occasionally one) might turn up their judgment at the tourist-thirst of some of the gentrified spaces, the occasional look of a mere outdoor shopping mall crowded with cute, promotional, profitable. Most of the time, the relative avoidance of slavery to the automobile,

Above, and above right: Every May the "Bay to Breakers" race attracts more than 100,000 runners, watchers, and other celebrants. Costumes have become a mainstay of the events and prizes are awarded for the best.

158

the imprisonment within watery boundaries, means that San Francisco avoids the look of an agglomerated megalopolis. As Spinoza said, freedom consists in knowing what the limits are. There may be crazies in the streets, but at least the streets are not barren freeways. The air is swept by the winds through the Golden Gate. The smog is beyond the hills and over there—across the bay in Oakland.

The city tends to regenerate itself and fight back. Freeway revolts, high-rise ordinances, anti-smoking campaigns don't always triumph, but sometimes they do. Change is not always for the worse. Take, for example, the old Haight-Ashbury, the land of acid dreams during the summer of love. Has it settled back into its prehistory of an easygoing San Francisco neighborhood, or kept its sad postrevolutionary role as America's first teenage slum, a troubled and dangerous ghetto, or has it been gentrified into still another Old Town, Union Street, Shopping Mall Eightiesland?

None of the above. The Haight has not been redeemed entirely, but it is becoming one of the great slightly eccentric, yet attractive all-American neighborhoods—a mixture of Orientals, blacks, gays, young families, and students on the old foundation of working-class San Francisco.

During the beatnik era of North Beach, Bunny Simon—a stately, slow-moving, and courtly Creole gentleman from New Orleans—presided over a talk and poetry hangout called The Anxious Asp. The North Beach saloon establishment didn't take to a man of color running a bar on its turf and he was forced out. Now Bunny Simon parks his wife's Rolls-Royce, a gift from him in honor of her Creole cooking, in front of his popular bar on Haight Street.... The Anxious Asp returns! Besides presiding over this establishment, he is writing a book. Sometimes I drop in to discuss it with him, along with one of his favorite novelists, Ernest Gaines, author of the prizewinning novel and film *The Autobiography of Miss Jane Pittman.* Everything changes; yet some things remain the same.

Many things are better in the Haight. During the period of litter, dope, and turmoil, the Haight-Ashbury shared with New York's East Village a dubious distinction: middle-class wrack and ruin. The neighborhood organized; business people and residents dug in. Now it is one of the truly integrated neighborhoods, every which way—black and white, gay and straight, stu-

dent and elderly, single and familied, poor and up-up-upwardly mobile. If not a Gold Coast Old Town, it's a Credit Coast Newville. The revived district has taken its place as a strolling, dining, shopping, cafe-sitting, moderately level-headed—but only moderately—cappuccino, croissant, quiche, book-and-record, Tiffany glass, health emporium, exercise studio, urban settlement. Some of the barber shops are not beauty parlors. There may be more Hunan cooking than is absolutely required, but there are also corner groceries. Less chic than Union Street or downtown San Francisco, the gentry of the Haight retain just a soupçon of laidback from ancient flower times.

Recently I spoke with a young woman at the Red Victorian cafe and cinema who said she used to be a street person, a dropout, but now she has straightened out her life and is going back to school to get her master's degree. "In what subject?" I asked.

"Holistics and Astrology," she said.

Since flaky remains a fact of life—although life is real and earnest, here as everywhere—it's better to accept the special atmosphere. Asked the word for a body of water entirely surrounded by land, a Marin County child answered, "Hot tub?" The proprietor of Fabulous Faces offers "caviar facials." After the dancer wife of a pianist ran off briefly with one of his musician friends, the couple rented a hall to perform a dance celebrating the recementing of their marital bonds. The performance had three parts: "Fugue," "Interlude," and "Return." The pianist and the dancer took joint bows to mild applause and lived happily forever afterward, or at least until the next month and the fourth part: "Dissolution."

A large percentage of the population of San Francisco lives alone—divorced or never married or gay or just young and, like Dick Whittington, come to the great city to fulfill the imperatives of hope and desire. The streets form a kind of maxi-family for those uprooted from traditional families. For the visitor, San Francisco can be a way of testing another sometimes humorous, sometimes sensual, sometimes merely wasteful way of living. Along with the new biotechnology and computer industries in the Bay Area, a village economy, a financial concentration, San Francisco is the locale for its unique celebration of itself. Those who come to visit are welcome to join the chorus during intervals between their own recitatives concerning the future of America.

Although devoted to secular pursuits, the city displays religion in all its glory and variety. *Opposite:* An Eastern Orthodox Christmas Mass is celebrated at Holy Virgin Cathedral *(above),* with the Archbishop raising the cross *(below, right).* The Russian church has a wonderful gilded dome that can be seen all over the Richmond district. At Grace Cathedral on Nob Hill, the Episcopal Archbishop and assistants prepare for Easter celebration before the great east doors, copies of Ghiberti's bronze doors on the Cathedral Baptistry in Florence *(below, left). Above:* The city's first church, founded in 1776, was Mission Dolores. In its small cemetery are buried the first governor of Spanish California, several pioneers, two victims of the Vigilantes, and some of the 5,500 Mission Indians who died from measles and other epidemics.

Above: Lawn bowling in Golden Gate Park becomes an eccentric sport when done in white face.

Opposite, above: A corner of the old cemetery at the Presidio, founded by Anza in 1776, served as a pet cemetery for animals belonging to young refugees of the earthquake.

Opposite, below: The courtyard-playground of Garfield Elementary School sits at the foot of Coit Tower.

Above: An entire family on a North Beach outing.

Opposite: Just north of the Golden Gate Bridge the sands of Rodeo Beach, part of the Golden Gate National Recreation Area, attract thousands of sun worshippers.

The city's buildings, particularly Victorian houses, show exuberant faces to the world. Sometimes, however, they appear shy with their names, as the "1232" saloon on Vallejo in North Beach *(above)*. Tommy's Joynt, Geary and Van Ness *(opposite, above)*, features stew from ranch-grown buffalo. A shop in Noe Valley *(opposite, below)* is housed in the type of Victorian called "Romeo and Juliet" for the stairway-balconies between the bay windows.

Overleaf: Murals have been in style in the city since the 1930s. *Left, above:* Social Realist murals were executed by WPA artists in the lobby of Coit Tower on Telegraph Hill. *Left, below:* The painter of this 1967 Summer of Love flower mural in the Haight-Ashbury recently revitalized her work. *Right:* A work in progress on Alice Street, South of Market, celebrates Philippine culture.

Second overleaf: Vigorous murals by Hispanic artists in the Mission district contrast strangely with the Victorian buildings. Here it's hard to tell which gingerbread is real.

The ocean and bay are a constant background for variety of activities, whether hang-gliding off Fort Funston's bluffs *(opposite, above),* boardsailing off the Marina district *(opposite, below),* beachcombing at Baker Beach *(above),* or Sunday painting—with some imagination— near the Bay Bridge *(below).*

Above: Geologically speaking, the Golden Gate is a strait several miles long, with the Bridge spanning its narrowest section.

Opposite: This glorious, welcoming sight has greeted merchant marine crews and ocean yachtsmen, soldiers returning from war, and passengers on Hawaiian cruises for five decades.

San Francisco lies at the tip of a peninsula, and there are other peninsulas and islands in the bay: Tiburon *(above)*, a wealthy Marin peninsula, has an attached near-island, Belvedere *(opposite, below)*. On East Brother Island *(opposite, above)*, a former lighthouse has been converted into a bed-and-breakfast inn.

Overleaf: Fifty-footers "hit the line" in the waters off the St. Francis Yacht Club (whose officials are on the motorboat in foreground) to begin their biennial regatta.

Above: Montara Beach, one of a couple of dozen "pocket beaches" south of San Francisco.

Opposite, above: A surfer who made a fortune as a real estate developer lives in this houseboat at Sausalito. Docked here are several hundred floating houses, often architect-designed two-story residences that have never sailed anywhere.

Oppositte, below: The commercial fishing fleet has made its home at Fisherman's Wharf since the turn of the century; the first seafood restaurant dates to the twenties.

Overleaf: Seen from the Marin headlands, a thunderstorm (usually seen only once in a decade) lights up the city.

Above: Health food stores abound; here is one in Mill Valley, across the Golden Gate.

Left: Dungeness crab cocktails and San Francisco sourdough bread are two sidewalk specialties at Fisherman's Wharf.

Opposite: Saturday mornings at the big Farmers' Market on Alemany Boulevard, near the freeway interchange, is crowded with farmers from as far away as Santa Barbara and buyers seeking the cheapest, the freshest, the biggest—also the most exotic. Farmers grow many specialty fruits and vegetables for San Francisco's numerous ethnic communities. Restaurateurs buy their produce at a wholesale market not far away.

Overleaf, left: Considered the workhorse of Bay area bridges because of its heavy traffic, the Oakland Bay Bridge was badly damaged in the 1989 earthquake. But repairs were completed in the remarkably short time of two months and commuting was back to normal. *Overleaf, right:* The homes on bayside Tiburon and Belvedere are fabulously expensive.

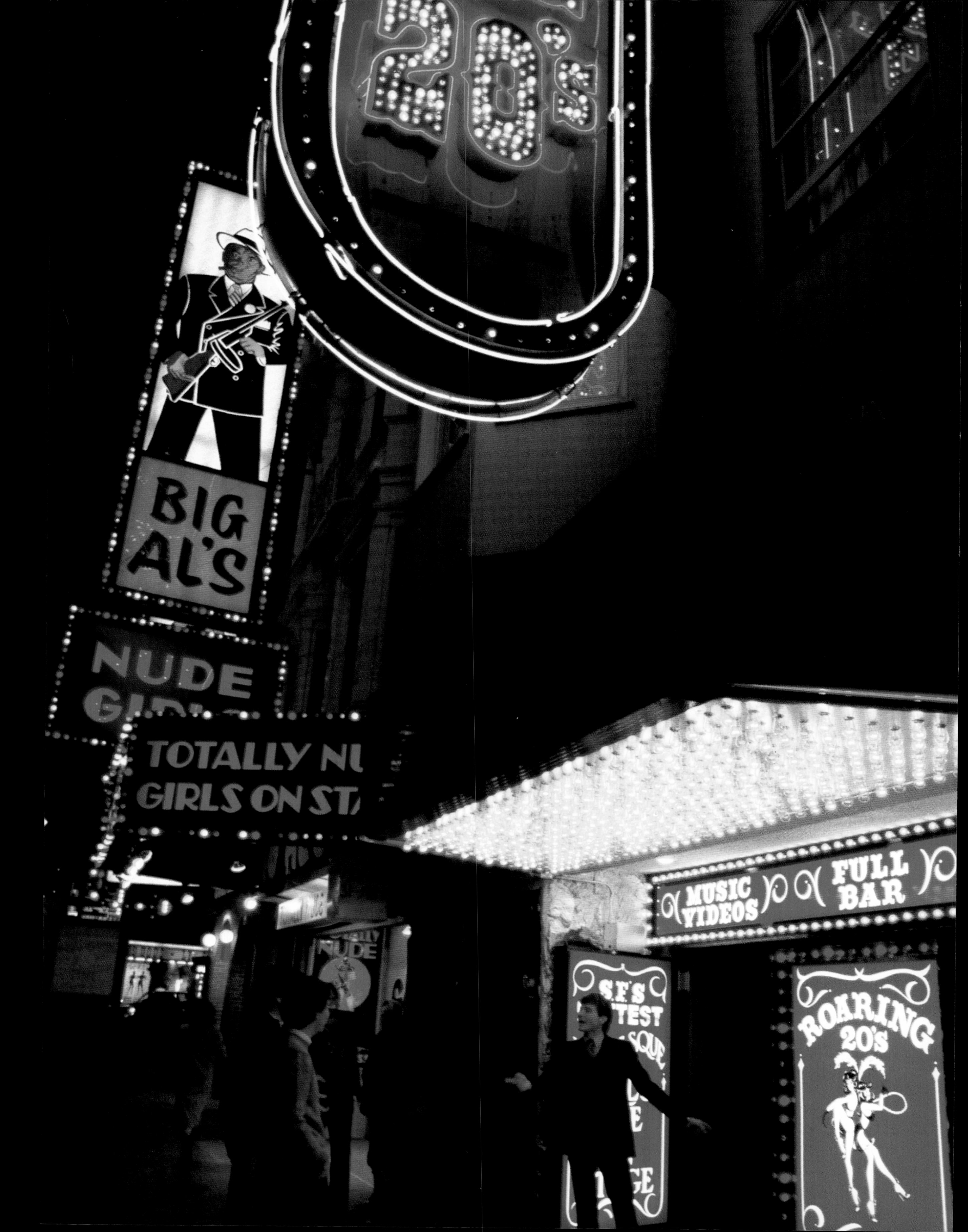
20's
BIG AL'S
NUDE
MUSIC VIDEOS
FULL BAR
ROARING 20's

NIGHTLIFE IN THE CITY

BY BARNABY CONRAD

At last count there were some 1,530 bars here—compared to 438 churches! San Francisco has always been a saloon and restaurant town and it has generally preferred ones with no-frills and no-nonsense decor about them, such as the Original Cold Day Restaurant, which, like the Poodle Dog, dates back to Gold Rush days. It is said that the Poodle Dog was originally named the Poulet d'Or but the first Pony Express rider couldn't pronounce it. This story, like the restaurant's food, should be taken *cum grano salis*.

I've been involved with San Francisco's nightlife since I was fifteen and did the murals in a popular nightclub on lower Broadway called the Tahitian Hut. Only a few months ago, I did a 35 × 11-foot mural in one of the city's elegant restaurants, Harris's on Van Ness Avenue.

In between, I owned three places. The most popular was El Matador, and perhaps by giving you some rambling, name-dropping memories of the place we can evoke some of the spirit of North Beach in those days before porn shops and girlie shows along Broadway.

It was midnight at El Matador in the mid-1950s, and there was a full moon, a night we usually expected any kooks that were abroad. Sinatra had just left, after picking up a spectacular woman with purplish hair at the bar. John Horton Cooper was behind the piano bar as always, his left hand marching up and down the keys in tenths on his great arrangement of "Sweet Lorraine." The usual complement of socialites was there, and John Clark (the Australian waiter) was having fun with a drunk at the bar around the big stuffed head of a bull on the wall—Maromero, the very bull that in the climactic scene of the film *Blood and Sand* was supposedly done in by Tyrone Power.

Broadway at Columbus is the Capitol of "Sin" Francisco.

"Hey," cried the inebriate, pointing a wavering finger at the bull, "tha' damned thing's alive—I jus' saw it breathe!"

He didn't know that some months before we had run a thin hose from the end of the bar down the length of the kitchen, through the wall and into the great hollow head of the bull to the nostrils. John Clark would blow a little smoke into his end of the hose from time to time—not too much, mind you—just enough to keep the drunk thinking he was losing his mind.

"Hey, barten'er, there it goes again," he gasped. "Looka tha' damn animal—'sbreathin'!"

Bill Edison, the gentle bartender, recently summa cum laude out of Amherst and of the wealthy shoe-manufacturing clan, pulled himself away from a conversation with sculptor Benny Bufano, adjusted his thick glasses, studied the bull's head solemnly, and announced in his quiet, scholarly way: "Really, sir, I see nothing out of the ordinary, simply a splendid example of a *Piedras Negras toro bravo* reasonably well taxidermed."

Of course, when Bill turned away another wisp of smoke, like a suggestion of ectoplasm, wafted down from the bull's muzzle. The drunk gulped his drink, paid up, and lurched out onto Broadway's teeming sidewalk, pale and shaking his head.

Earlier in the evening Niels Mortensen, who had started the place with me back in 1953, had experienced a slight contretemps with one of the waiters. We had thought we knew all the ways that one could be cheated in the bar business, but here was a new wrinkle. We'd been aware for some days that not all of the money paid by customers was showing up in the till at the end of the evening. We certainly knew the thief wasn't among our faithful bartenders nor our several longtime waiters. But for a week we'd had a new waiter, and when Niels heard him gurgle, the jig was up. It seems that the enterprising chap had hung two douche bags around his neck under his shirt: one filled with gin, the other scotch. And the hoses from each ran down his arms under his sleeves. He would get the ice and mixers himself from the end of the bar, spritz his own alcohol into the glass, and eliminate the necessity for a bartender and a cash register altogether. He was congratulated on his ingenuity by Niels and then firmly kicked out the back way into the parking lot and helped away by the lot attendant.

I was at the piano bar having a pleasant drink with my brother, Hunt, but the action seemed over for the evening. I was

Opposite, above: Mara's Bakery in North Beach is famous all over town.

Opposite, below: The elegant, new Pan Pacific Hotel fronts on Post Street.

thinking of driving home to Belvedere, when in came a blonde with a distinguished-looking man. I had met the woman, Eva Gabor, but it took me a moment to place the impeccable man in the Savile Row suit as Noel Coward. We were used to stars in El Matador, from Brando to Graham Greene to Sammy Davis, Jr., but somehow, when probably the greatest showman of them all was gracing our little establishment, I felt that El Matador had suddenly been promoted in status from saloon to salon by the touch of a magic wand. He was as witty and urbane as one would expect, and he looked at all the many taurine artifacts around the walls with great interest; he loved the four live macaws in their glass-enclosed aviary, he complimented me on my life-size painting of Manolete, he exclaimed about the 30 × 13-foot mural of the Seville bullring, he admired the original Picasso drawing, and he chortled appreciatively over the cartoon Charles Addams had done for us. (It depicted a bull standing smugly in the middle of the arena with the matador's ear at his feet.)

When Johnny Cooper asked if he'd honor us by playing, Noel graciously sat down, ran his fingers over the keys, and then not so graciously snapped: "In a lifetime of music, this is the most recalcitrant instrument I've ever had the misfortune to confront—it actually fights back!"

But he swung manfully into "I'll See You Again" and "Zigeuner" and other Coward standards, singing them and punctuating them with acerbic comments that had the people seated at the nearby tables in hysterics. I don't remember his witticisms, unfortunately, but I do recall a brief exchange between my brother and Miss Gabor.

Eva: "Bahnaby tells me you haf a vooden leg"—groping under the table—"which one iss it?"

Hunt: "Eva, I never thought I'd have to tell a Gabor what a man's leg feels like."

Eva: (a little loftily) "Vell, dahling, ve vass never in the lumber business!"

I remember that evening with great fondness. I won't say it was your typical night at "The Mat"—Sinatra and Gabor and Coward didn't come in every night of the week. On the other hand, it was not atypical. It seemed that there were very few dull evenings at 492 Broadway.

Why all the fuss about the place; why its constant popularity;

Cafferata Ravioli Factory, one of North Beach's many Italian restaurants, dates back to the last century. In the 1860s it was called "Tazzo D'Oro" (cup of gold, a very rich coffee), a name still memorialized on the window.

why do people still stop me on the street, say, "There never was a place like it," and urge me to recreate it? It was not a great restaurant, nor even much of a restaurant at all. Though we did have a kitchen with an actual stove in it, the space was used mostly for amorous dalliance and the making of liaisons between customers and employees—a good deal of which, I am informed reliably, went on. If food was urgently required; if say, Eartha Kitt or Paul Newman or Judy Garland absolutely had to have a sandwich, a waiter would scurry next door to Vanessi's and get them one. For one year, we actually had a quite splendid buffet luncheon that was cooked off the premises by our manager. But all that food in the kitchen got in the way of the dalliances and the liaisons, and we gave it up and went back to being what we started out to be in the first place: an oxymoron, a contradiction in terms—an elegant saloon.

Maybe that's why it was successful, because it was elegant. And yet it kept its saloon flavor in a very San Franciscan and Barbary Coast type of setting. We had no entertainment except Cooper, who was hired before the place was created and who stayed at his same piano bar for the eleven years that I owned it. Along the line, at different periods, the great bassists Vernon Alley and George Butterfield backed up Cooper. We also had many guests who would drop in for relaxation and noodle around on the piano—such immortals as Art Tatum, Duke Ellington, Vince Guaraldi, Hoagy Carmichael, Joe Bushkin, Errol Garner, George Shearing, and Bobby Short. We also never quite knew what other kinds of entertainers might feel like performing after their stints elsewhere: Jose Greco, for example, suddenly getting up and dancing on top of the piano bar; Elaine May and Mike Nichols trying out a new routine; Johnny Mathis singing along with Cooper; or—night of nights—when Lenny Bruce from up the street at Ann's 440 Club and Jonathan Winters from down the street at Banducci's hungry i engaged in a verbal battle—and it was that—to see who could be funnier. The contest was never totally resolved, but the customers lucky enough to be there at the time became limp from an hour of constant laughter. If I'm not mistaken, that was also the night that Winters blew his stack, climbed the rigging of the *Balclutha*, and was taken away for a long rest at the "funny farm," as he referred to it afterward.

Opposite: Cafe Roma, a familiar and popular coffeehouse-restaurant, opens a welcoming window along Columbus Avenue in the North Beach area.

Overleaf: "Bawdway," as Herb Caen would say, forms a raucous boundary zone between North Beach and Chinatown. Here is part of a monumental neon sign, "NUDE."

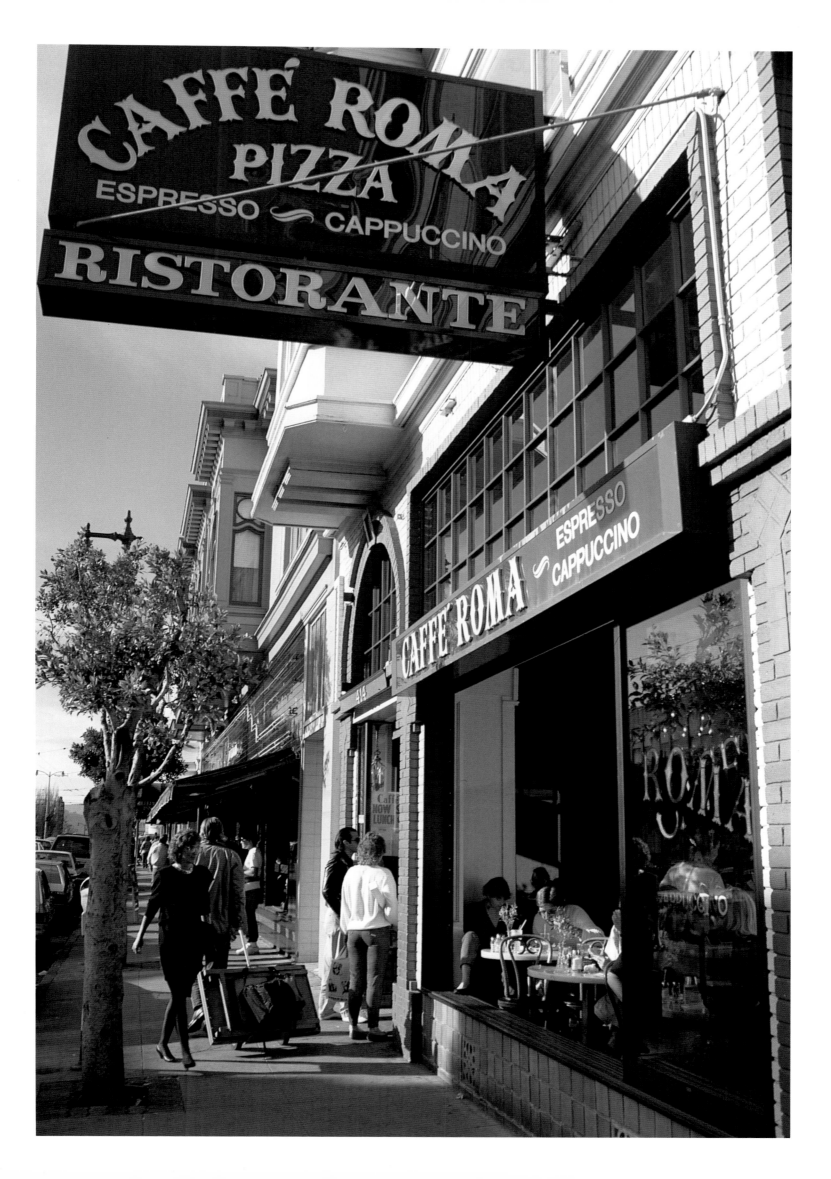

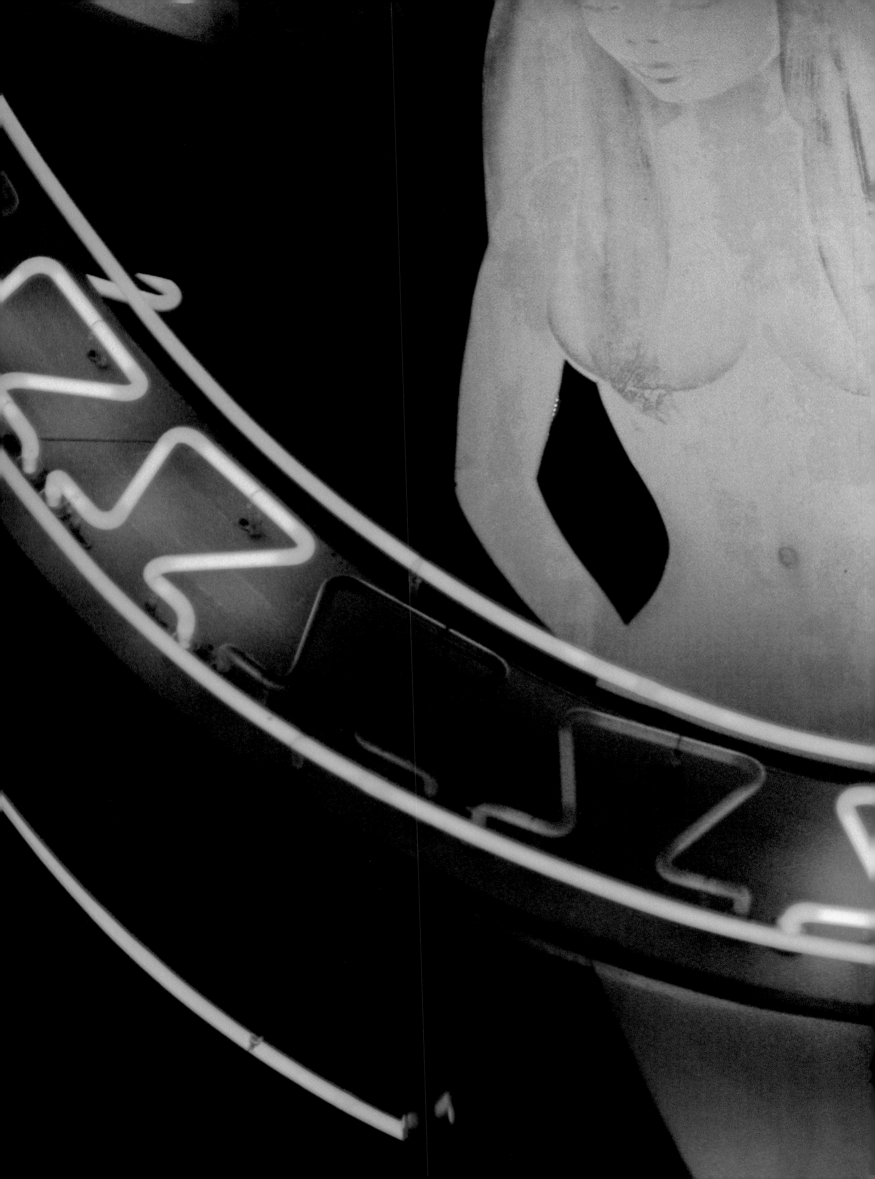

Above: Elite Cafe, featuring Creole delights, stands among several flourishing restaurants on Fillmore Street, between Pacific Heights and the Marina.

Opposite: Bentley's, a seafood restaurant with oyster bar, offers modern-day etched glass as an echo of long-lost, grand-style restaurants.

198

Another unique form of entertainment: on Sundays we would show bullfighting films, which I would narrate while the redoubtable guitarist Juan Buckingham played Tarrega and Albeniz in the background.

A peripheral entertainment at the Matador was the men's room. In an attempt to avoid the usual cretinous graffiti found in most such places, we made the entire room a blackboard and encouraged creativity by providing lots of chalk in trays. The visitors responded enthusiastically, and rarely a day went by that we didn't find some little gem. Even Jack, our splendid janitor (and guitarist, writer, and rare bird lover), got in the act. He drew an arena filled with cheering bulls in the stands and in the ring a bull expertly caping a charging man. Underneath was:

> When earth's last *olé* is over
> on the shining sands tomorrow—
> Toros will Toreros be,
> Toreros will be toros.

We couldn't bear to erase it so that one was painted permanently in white lines. Another verse that was there for a long time was written by Robert Mitchum; I made a note of it—and am still trying to figure it out:

> Compadre—when all the broken crockery of
> desperate communion is swept from under our
> understanding heels we may find on that clear
> expanse of floor the true and irrevocable
> target of infinite trust.

That one was transferred to our fancy guest album. As I leaf through the yellow, smoke-scented pages of that book I see that it is quite a record of the decade. A young Ronald Reagan, Governor Pat Brown, mobster Mickey Cohen, and Mary Martin seemed to have been there the same week as S. I. Hayakawa, Rita Hayworth, and Aly Kahn. On one page, Peter Hurd did a charming New Mexico scene in watercolor (he carried a miniature set of colors in his pocket). And, of course, Dong Kingman's handsome drawing is no surprise. But the clever sketches by John Huston, Ingrid Bergman, Ray Bolger, José Ferrer, and Tom Harmon are not expected. I well remember the day Tyrone Power came in, because after I admired his gold cuff links, he sent them to me the next day. (Do people do that sort of thing today?) And then there were the great writers whose names

Opposite, above: The Cadillac Bar, discreetly located at the intersection of two South of Market alleys, attracts attention for its Mexican food and giant props.

Opposite, below: One of the four oldest restaurants in the city, Schroeder's (1893) features authentic German cuisine and weekly Bavarian dancing.

Overleaf, left: The new Marriott Hotel, affectionately called the "Jukebox," faces the Moscone Center and, not surprisingly, has become one of the largest convention hotels in the city.

Overleaf, right: Atop Nob Hill sits the famous Mark Hopkins Inter-Continental Hotel, with its "Top of the Mark" room.

grace the book: John Steinbeck, Erskine Caldwell, and Irwin Shaw, among others.

But Bill Edison was dissatisfied. "I came to San Francisco and became a bartender because I read *The Time of Your Life*, and the bar business isn't much like that play and I haven't even seen William Saroyan and I think I'll go back to St. Louis." Since Bill was our best bartender, I kept hoping that one night the legendary Saroyan would indeed come in, but he had long since left San Francisco and was living in Paris.

Then, one miraculous night, accompanied by Herb Caen, in strolled the mustachioed, ebullient writer. But it was Bill Edison's night off! I tried to keep the great man entertained while Niels frantically tracked Bill down. He was finally found in a movie theater and rushed to the Matador, just as Saroyan was leaving. The author was impressed with Bill's knowledge and insights into his writings; they talked far into the night, and a happy Bill stayed on as bartender. (He later became a teacher and is now a distinguished educator.)

In similar fashion, a black Coast Guardsman named Alex Haley used to come in to talk books with Niels and me. We were the only writers he had ever met. He yearned to be a writer, though the only money he had ever made with his typewriter was from love letters that he would write at a dollar each for his less articulate shipmates. He had a trunkful of rejection slips for his work, but felt he had a great book in him about his family and thought that by hanging around us he could learn "the trick."

One night a really successful writer came in—Budd Schulberg, fresh from his Oscar-winning *On the Waterfront* and his play *Disenchanted*. I phoned Alex; luckily he was in town, and he got himself over from Oakland in about three minutes. He and Schulberg talked writing until six in the morning; they became friends, and Alex was inspired as never before.

I don't apologize for this being the name-droppingest article because it was the name-droppingest place; people went there to see and be seen. Samuel Johnson once said that a good public house was one of God's noblest creations, and in a city of historically great saloons, El Matador must be included. Originally, it was an Italian dance cafe called The Castle View (though what view of what castle one never knew). I bought it in 1953 with some of the loot my best-selling novel *Matador* was reaping. I

had started the place for fun and frolic, not money, and I had a ball while it lasted. But finally, after eleven years or so of it, I wearied of the game, sold the place, and went to Tahiti.

My last act at El Matador was to find a nice home for the four beautiful macaws that had spent a decade in their glass aviary at the end of the bar. I offered them to the Santa Barbara Zoo, which accepted the gift gratefully with a letter saying that before the birds arrived they wanted "to duplicate their previous environment exactly" and asking me to please describe it in detail.

"Get a piano player with a good stride bass," I began my reply, "add about forty people in various stages of intoxication, place in a dark, noisy, smoke-filled enclosure with a lot of laughter, and then...."

El Matador is no more, just as the Tahitian Hut, Ann's 440, where Johnny Mathis started, and the hungry i, where Streisand, Woody Allen, and others started, are no more.

But a block away from where El Matador used to be, people still line up, as they have for four decades, to see the drag show at Finochio's. (Herb Caen once wrote: "Joe Finochio is the only person who lives off the labor of his fruits.") And nearby are the jammed Washington Square Bar and Grill and Enrico's Sidewalk Cafe, and not too far away is the elegant, if stuffy, Venetian Room of the Fairmont Hotel with its headliner performers; and there are dozens of newer, colorful places waiting to be discovered around town.

For as long as there is a San Francisco the city will have its nightlife—just as sure as the sun goes down.

Above: Nob Hill's Fairmont Hotel, one of the grandest old hostelries, has a huge, magnificently overdecorated red, gold, and black lobby that a luxury liner could berth in.

Overleaf: Viewed from Bush Street, the Russ Building (left foreground) stands as one of the city's most beautiful architectural landmarks, somewhat dwarfed but not overshadowed by new highrise construction.

THE REDISCOVERED SHORE

BY JOHN HART

Above: a windsurfer takes to the water beneath the Golden Gate Bridge. Bay water temperatures mandate wet suits all year round.

Opposite: The square-rigged Balclutha now rests at the National Maritime Museum at Hyde Street Pier.

Location, as they say, is everything. Even more than most cities, San Francisco is the product of a place, and the place is the Golden Gate. To that flooded rift in the hills the city owes its existence, its history, and much of the lively jumble of its present character.

In these days of airports and bridges it is easy to forget how special the Golden Gate has always been: the one decent opening in a thousand miles of forbidding coast; the portal to the greatest natural harbor in the West. When the Gold Rush brought the world pouring through that door, the unimpressive town that huddled nearby was turned overnight into a gatekeeper city: welcomer, hosteler, supplier, entertainer—and guardian; for the Americans, like the Spanish and Mexicans before them, lined the strategic strait with fortifications and guns.

Time has left visible marks on the land and invisible ones on the water. Look at the right kind of map and you'll see that the city limits of San Francisco in fact take in the entire Golden Gate, right up to tideline on the Marin Headlands. They include also Alcatraz Island, Yerba Buena-Treasure Island, and odd colonial footholds on the shores of neighboring counties. (The Farallon Islands, twenty miles outside the Gate, are San Franciscan too.) Even today, all ships entering San Francisco Bay run through city waters, if no longer under the muzzles of San Francisco guns.

The city has never quite lost its gatekeeper role, its salty maritime imprint. If the modern town is no longer queen of Pacific commerce, it still faces outward, as well as self-absorbedly inward; and it still possesses one of the most diverting, and most accessible shorelines of any city in the world.

The preservation of this shoreline is something of a miracle. It so easily could have been fumbled away. Indeed, for a time after World War II, the city seemed to turn its back on the water. The commercial port went into a long decline. The military lands along the shore were threatened with disposal and development. The city's own waterfront parks were increasingly run-down and sad, and inadequate sewage treatment left near-shore waters reeking.

There was a tendency (not quite gone today) to treat the waterfront as a sacrifice area, a place to put whatever the feisty inland neighborhoods rejected. Freeways, for instance. In the 1950s, the plan was to connect the Bay and Golden Gate Bridges with an elevated expressway. It would wrap around the salty edge of town, dropping a concrete curtain in front of the Ferry Building, Fisherman's Wharf, Fort Mason, the Marina, the Presidio bay coastline—landmark after landmark.

But only a mile or so of the infamous Embarcadero Freeway was built before the nation's first Freeway Revolt chopped it off, leaving an awkward stub end hanging for three decades in front of Pier 7. (It was all finally torn down in 1992.)

The Freeway Revolt of the 1960s marks the start of a great revival. Since then the city and its citizens (with a lot of help from the feds) have made an astonishing effort to reclaim, rebuild, and open up the briny urban border: to take advantage of it, indeed, as never before. Today:

• The former military bases clustered at the Golden Gate have all become federal parkland: the Golden Gate National Recreation Area (GGNRA). The resulting greenbelt covers almost all of the city's ocean coast and much of its northern waterfront as well. It includes also the bay islands, Alcatraz and Angel; the Marin Headlands, northern wall of the Gate; and other lands sprawling far north into Marin County and far south into San Mateo County. The GGNRA today is the most heavily visited federal park in the United States.

• A stop has been put to the filling of San Francisco Bay to make real estate, a process that goes back to the Fortyniners and once threatened to reduce the great harbor to a constricted channel. Anything built on the waterfront today must have a reason for being, specifically, there. San Francisco voters have ruled that even hotels must keep a respectful distance.

Above, and right, below: The legendary prison, Alcatraz, with Angel Island State Park in the background.

At right, above: The dramatic cliffs north of the Point Bonita Lighthouse form part of the Golden Gate National Recreation Area.

San Francisco Fire Department crews and volunteers from the Presidio combat the fires in the Marina District during the 1989 earthquake. *Photo courtesy Presidio Museum*

• The Port of San Francisco, after years of decline, seems to be on a modest rebound as an international cargo terminal. The Port's "Lost Coast" south of the Ferry Building, dilapidated for years, seems headed for a rambunctious renaissance.

• It took an earthquake to do it, but the Embarcadero Freeway is finally, actually, gone. Once more the Ferry Building, headquarters of the Port, is at the center of the view down Market Street, as intended from the beginning.

Location: Fort Mason, overlooking the inner vestibule of the Golden Gate, has a dandy one. The Spanish sited cannon on its heights. In American hands it was a conduit for war supplies and troops (one and a half million soldiers shipped out from its three big piers during World War II alone). Today, Fort Mason is the headquarters of the federal arc-of-parks and the site of a cultural complex perhaps unique in the world.

The new thing that has taken shape in these piers and wharfside buildings goes by a jaw-cracking title: The Fort Mason Center for the Arts, Humanities, Recreation, Education and Ecology. What's offered here is not some centralized program, but something more precious: *space.* Space for offices, classes, galleries, museums; places to rehearse and places to perform; halls for exhibits and halls for conferences—300,000 square feet in all, and still growing.

The smaller niches at Fort Mason, in the five "forepier" buildings, are the quarters of some fifty resident nonprofit groups, from the Oceanic Society to the ItaloAmerican Museum, from the Blue Bear School of Music to Western Public Radio. They pay rent, but less than they would anywhere else. It's not surprising that a hundred more such outfits are waiting for a vacancy.

The barnlike buildings on the piers offer much bigger realms, including two sizeable halls and one very well-equipped midsize theater, available for every kind of event from flower shows to an exposition of the "anatriptic arts." Five hundred groups use these facilities each year; again, many more would like to.

You can get, at Fort Mason, a hot dog or a gourmet vegetarian meal. You can take your pick of five art galleries and five theatres. You can go to a lecture, a circus, or an opera composed last year. You can take up writing, painting, or computing; you can do your bit to save the world or the whales. There's a special emphasis on things that kids can do with their adults.

Loosely in charge of this nonprofit bustle is the nonprofit Fort Mason Foundation. The Foundation, created for this purpose, maintains the buildings and decides which activities to house. It looks, among other things, for maximum variety. "A lot of the breadth comes naturally," says Executive Director Marc Kasky. "The pieces come to us." The Foundation gets its $1.5 million annual budget from rents; government money has been out of the picture for years.

What's to be done with the military complexes all around the country that are shutting down and falling into local hands? Will they benefit local economies, or burden them? What will they be good for? The example of Fort Mason—already imitated elsewhere in the Golden Gate National Recreation Area—suggests one lively answer.

Not far east of Fort Mason the federal waterfront ends and the city takes charge. (The worlds overlap at Hyde Street Pier, which the National Park Service leases for some of its historic ships.) The next 7.4 miles, curving around and down to Hunter's Point, constitute the Port of San Francisco.

In the middle of that arc is the Ferry Building. Constructed in 1898, it was once the largest building in California; for much longer than that it was the hub of the water-based metropolitan transportation system from which it took its name. The transbay bridges, built in the 1930s, pretty well took care of that. After 1958 the Embarcadero Freeway slashed across the building's front yard, seeming to underline the lesson: pavement matters in transportation; water doesn't.

Now, with the freeway gone, the Ferry Building seems subtly to recover its old importance. That may reflect a reality. Ferries, indeed, are back, and slowly regaining ridership. The water roads do matter.

As headquarters of the Port of San Francisco, the Ferry Building witnesses considerable tension. Running the port is an endless balancing act. Unlike other city departments, this one is expected to pay its own way. It does so from "wharfage, dockage and demurrage," commercial and maritime rentals, and a few other sources. It is under constant pressure to make money. At the same time the public sees its waterfront more and more as an amenity to be opened up and cherished, profit or no. The tension, a Port Commission member remarks, "keeps us in a fair amount of trouble."

Out of these pressures, against all odds, there seems to be evolving something rather fine: a money-making, cargo-handling, tourist-enticing, salty, fishy, generally handsome conglomeration that does the city proud.

One kind of vitality is apparent north of the Ferry Building, where the piers carry odd numbers. This is the world of Fisherman's Wharf, ferry and cruise ship terminals, and touristy Pier 39, recently invaded and superbly advertised by a colony of sea lions. More traditional port functions—cotton warehouse, newsprint pier—are concealed behind distinctive, uniform facades.

The recreational zone is now spreading south of the Ferry Building, into the even-numbered region. Several old piers have been removed outright (at a cost of a million dollars apiece) to open a waterside promenade; just south of the Bay Bridge, there are plans for a major new cruise terminal with lavish incidentals.

A grittier kind of energy shows at the southernmost edge of the Port's domain, down on piers 80 and 96—if you can call these broad expanses "piers." They seem rather to belong at an airport. Modern maritime commerce has little use for slim traditional "finger-piers," fringing the shore like cilia. What's needed now is *room*.

These days most goods that travel by sea, whatever their par-

Above: A Spanish cannon from the Castillo de San Joaquin captures the imagination of a young visitor to the Presidio Army Museum.

Opposite, above: Built in 1863, the Old Station Hospital, oldest complete building in the Presidio, now houses the Presidio Army Museum.

Opposite, below: An aerial view of the Presidio, founded by the Spanish in 1776 and in continuous use as a military base for more than 200 years. This longest-serving base in the United States has been converted into a National Park, under the auspices of the Golden Gate National Recreation Area.

Overleaf: In the foreground is Fort Mason, the major jumping-off point for American troops bound for the Pacific theater in World War II. Now a non-profit center for the arts, Fort Mason's buildings house galleries, theaters, workshops, and offices for performing arts, cultural, and conversation groups.

ticular shapes and sizes, get packed in uniform metal containers about the size of trucks. Stevedoring today consists of moving these in and out of ships, at an amazing clip, with the help of enormous cranes. Wharfside, stacks of containers pile up, waiting for the next stage in their journey: another ship, perhaps, a train, or a trailer-truck.

Some ports modernized quickly when this new technology loomed; San Francisco was one that delayed, missing, literally, the boat. But the Port is playing a successful game of catch up now.

It's hard for the public to get very close to these monster operations; from a distance you notice just the cranes, looking like strange stick insects, their function not very clear. Seen closer to, they crouch at the water's edge like science-fictional invaders, their great working arms extended over vessels or, when not in use, stored vertically. Around them are acres of stacked containers, empty or laden, labeled Nedlloyd or Evergreen, Cosco or Zim: the Netherlands, Taiwan, mainland China, Israel.

Many of these loads are going on east by rail, and here the city has an advantage some of its competitors lack: tracks running to wharfside. Containers can be shifted to freight cars here without an intermediate trip by truck on busy public streets. A pier with a railroad on it, by the way, isn't just a pier: it is an Intermodal Container Transfer Facility.

It's hard not to root for the survival of the oldest port on the west coast of the United States, not just as a tourist attraction but as a link in the waterborne commerce of the world. Take that element away, and wouldn't everything else these coastlines have to offer—fishing boats and tourist spots, seagulls and sea lions, recreation and history, cultures and cuisines—seem just perceptibly less real?

Opposite: A Fort Mason pier building hosts an international children's fair.

Left, above: An artist's rendering shows how the Mission Bay Development will look upon completion. A city within a city, the project will provide 8,700 new homes surrounded by sixty-eight acres of public parks and open space with shops, restaurants and a low-rise office district.

Left, below: The twenty-two acres of the Yerba Buena Gardens Redevelopment Project incorporates the Moscone Convention Center, the Center for the Arts/Performing Arts Theater, the Center for the Arts/Visual Arts Building, and the San Francisco Museum of Modern Art.

At right, top and middle: Following the earthquake of 1989, Pier 39's yacht harbor was invaded by seals. More than a hundred now make the docks their homes, sharing landing space with pleasure boats and commuter ferries. Seals and pups that require special care are treated at the Marine Mammal Center in the Marin headlands.

At right, below: The Port of San Francisco harbors two major container terminals, a sophisticated hub for relaying containers between vessels bound for Latin and South America and the Far East. Participants in the Mission Bay project, the Port will expand as work proceeds.

Overleaf: Fully laden, a container ship passes east of the city toward the Port of San Francisco.

*This book is dedicated
to my father, Morton C. Beebe*

For their generous advice and help in
producing this book I would like to thank
Robert Morton, my editor at Harry N.
Abrams, Inc., designer Judith Michael, and
revision coordinator Jean M. Berg.

Project Director: Robert Morton
Art Direction and Design: Judith Michael
Editor: Beverly Fazio

New Revised Edition 1993

Library of Congress Cataloging in Publication Data
Beebe, Morton.
San Francisco.
1. San Francisco (Calif.)—Description—Views.
1. Caen, Herb, 1916–   .   II. Title.
F869.S343B43   1985   979.4´61   85–4083
ISBN 0–8109–3834–0

The publisher wishes to thank the following
individuals and institutions for permission
to reproduce historic and other illustrations:
Society of California Engineers; Society of California Pioneers;
California Historical Society; San Francisco Maritime National
Historic Park; Carl Wilmington; View by View; Tracy Walklet;
Terra-Mar with Hewlett-Packard.